# Innovative Ideas for School Business Officials

## Best Practices from ASBO's Pinnacle Awards

Edited by David A. Ritchey

Published in partnership with the
Association of School Business Officials International

SCARECROWEDUCATION
Lanham, Maryland • Toronto • Oxford
2004

Published in the United States of America
by ScarecrowEducation
An imprint of The Rowman & Littlefield Publishing Group, Inc.
4501 Forbes Boulevard, Suite 200, Lanham, Maryland 20706
www.scarecroweducation.com

PO Box 317
Oxford
OX2 9RU, UK

British Library Cataloguing in Publication Information Available

**Library of Congress Cataloging-in-Publication Data**

Innovative ideas for school business officials : best practices from
ASBO's Pinnacle awards / edited by David A. Ritchey.
      p.   cm.
   "Published in partnership with the Association of School Business
Officials International."
   ISBN 1-57886-086-5 (pbk. : alk. paper)
   1. Public schools—United States—Business management   2. School
business administrators—United States.   I. Ritchey, David A., 1949–   II.
Association of School Business Officials International.
LB2823.5 .I56   2004
371.2′06—dc22                                            2003019922

∞ ™ The paper used in this publication meets the minimum
requirements of American National Standard for Information
Sciences—Permanence of Paper for Printed Library Materials,
ANSI/NISO Z39.48-1992. Manufactured in the United States
of America.

# Contents

# *Foreword*

School business officials all over the world must deal with two major challenges: (1) increased accountability in education and (2) tightening budgets. One or the other of these challenges alone would be significant; together they create an extraordinary circumstance.

Few people would argue with the notion that all children should be educated to high levels and that schools should be held accountable for doing everything they can to make that a reality. And few people would argue that school districts shouldn't use the resources they have in the most efficient and effective way possible. But as both educators and policy-makers point out, the devil is in the detail. When one set of policies requires that school districts implement regulations to raise the achievement of all children, and at the same time policies to provide the resources to do so are lacking, then new ideas, action, and change must occur.

My observation is that school business officials, in general, have a "can do," solutions-oriented approach to their role. They tend to use data to make decisions and they bring objectivity to problem solving in a way that other leaders in the district sometimes cannot. Because of these characteristics, the role of the school business official is becoming more important than it has ever been. The goal of all children reaching their greatest potential in school will not happen without the effective allocation of resources—or, in these tight economic times, the effective *reallocation* of resources. School business officials are key to making that happen.

Models have always been one of the best teachers. The *ASBO International Pinnacle Awards Program* was established by the Association of School Business Officials International to create models by recognizing outstanding practices and new ideas that result in significant contributions to school entities, the profession of school business, or to ASBO International and its affiliates. What has resulted from the program over the last 19 years is a growing set of ideas, replicable in other school districts. Those presented here are meant to inspire action and change—which will result in the most effective utilization of resources possible, so all children can be educated to high levels of achievement.

We are most grateful to Virco Manufacturing Corporation for their commitment to excellence in school business through their support of the Pinnacle Awards Program since 1993. Together we hope the pages of this book will become "dog eared" from use. And we hope the implementation of ideas presented here will inspire the creation of new practices, which can, in turn, be shared through the Pinnacle Awards Program.

Anne Miller, Ph.D., Executive Director,
Association of School Business Officials International

# Introduction

School business officials are known for their innovative, meaningful contributions to the improvement of their profession and the efficiency of school entities. The ASBO International Pinnacle Awards were established to recognize outstanding practices and new ideas that result in significant contributions to school entities. Successful applications have focused on areas such as budgeting, construction, cost savings, energy conservation, resource reallocation, safety, transportation, and technology.

The profiles of Pinnacle Award applications in this book are intended to provide school business officials with specific ideas to save money or improve processes in a variety of areas related to the day-to-day operation of schools. The money and time saved by implementing these ideas can then be applied where it is needed most, whether for classroom instruction, additional teacher preparation, or other human resources needs, to guarantee that all students are taught by highly qualified professionals, to balance budgets in maintenance or other areas, or to replenish a rainy day fund. As one of the applicants said, utilizing ideas here may help school business officials to do "what is best for the children."

Several tables are provided to help you find solutions for your needs. Table 1.1 organizes the profiles in this book by areas for which school business officials are generally responsible. The areas include transportation management, technology and technological innovations, internal operations, facilities management (including maintenance and construction/renovation management), energy management and energy efficiency, human resources management, purchasing, safety, and food service. Profiles in each area are marked with an "x."

Table 1.2 uses information from the National Center for Education

**Table 1.1   Profiles by Subject Area**

| Profile | Trans-portation | Tech-nology | Internal Operations | Fac. Mgt. | Energy | H.R. | Purch. | Safety | Food Svc. |
|---|---|---|---|---|---|---|---|---|---|
| School Bus Tracking and Safety (p. 1) | x | | | | | | | | |
| Electronic Solution for Print Shop (p. 5) | | x | x | | | | | | |
| Implementing Change in Facilities Management (p. 11) | | x | | x | | | | | |
| Creating a District-Wide Energy Management Program (p. 19) | x | | | | x | | | | |
| Human Resources Department Web Access (p. 25) | | x | | | | x | | | |
| Purchasing Department Website (p. 31) | | x | | | | | x | | |
| Emergency Preparedness/Response CD ROM (p. 37) | | x | | | | | | x | |
| School Construction Institute (p. 41) | | | x | x | | | | | |
| District-Wide Networked Connected Digital Copier Solution Integrated with a School-to-Career Program (p. 45) | | x | x | | | | | | |
| Design and Construction Database Linked to Photographic Documentation (p. 51) | | x | | x | | | | | |
| Redesign of Secondary School Reimbursable Meals Program: "Maxi-Meals" (p. 55) | | | | | | | | | x |
| Meeting Pupil Transportation Challenges through Cooperation and Innovation (p. 61) | x | | | | | | | | |
| Primary Vendor Contract for Maintenance Supplies (p. 67) | | | | | | | x | | |
| District Energy Program Reaps Multiple Rewards (p. 73) | | | x | x | x | | | | |
| Building Mentoring Program (p. 79) | | | | | | x | | | |
| Superintendent's Building Excellence Program (p. 83) | | | | x | | | | | |

**Table 1.2 Profiles by CCD Information**

| Profile | 0–50 Schools | More than 50 schools | Under 100 "other" staff | 100–500 "other" staff | Over 500 "other" staff | Expenditures under $50 mil. | Expenditures $50–$100 mil. | Expenditures over $100 mil. | NA (Can./BOCES) |
|---|---|---|---|---|---|---|---|---|---|
| School Bus Tracking and Safety (p. 1) | x | | | x | | x | | | |
| Electronic Solution for Print Shop (p. 5) | | | | | | | | | x |
| Implementing Change in Facilities Management (p. 11) | x | | | | x | | | x | |
| Creating a District-Wide Energy Management Program (p. 19) | x | | | | x | | | x | |
| Human Resources Department Web Access (p. 25) | | x | | | | | | | x |
| Purchasing Department Website (p. 31) | | | | | x | | | x | |
| Emergency Preparedness/Response CD ROM (p. 37) | x | | | | x | | | x | |
| School Construction Institute (p. 41) | x | | | x | | x | | | |
| District-Wide Networked Connected Digital Copier Solution Integrated with a School-to-Career Program (p. 45) | x | | | x | | x | | | |
| Design and Construction Database Linked to Photographic Documentation (p. 51) | x | | | x | | x | | | |
| Redesign of Secondary School Reimbursable Meals Program: "Maxi-Meals" (p. 55) | | x | | | x | | | x | |
| Meeting Pupil Transportation Challenges through Cooperation and Innovation (p. 61) | | | | | | | | | x |
| Primary Vendor Contract for Maintenance Supplies (p. 67) | x | | | | x | | x | | |
| District Energy Program Reaps Multiple Rewards (p. 73) | x | | | x | | x | | | |
| Building Mentoring Program (p. 79) | x | | | x | | | x | | |
| Superintendent's Building Excellence Program (p. 83) | x | | | | x | | | | |

Statistics (NCES) Common Core of Data (CCD), which includes number of students, size of budget, etc. Each profile in this book contains information from the CCD, including number of schools in the district, number of students, "locale/code" (there are eight codes, ranging from large central city to rural), total staff, "other staff" (staff excluding classroom teachers), and total 2001–2002 expenditures. Thus you can learn about the characteristics of the school districts that have implemented the innovations described and compare your own school district to the profiles. Note that Canadian districts and the BOCES profile included here do not have CCD data available.

School business officials and others involved with educational administration are encouraged to apply for ASBO's Pinnacle Awards to be recognized for programs or innovations which have improved their school districts' effectiveness or efficiency. For additional information and an application form, visit ASBO's website at www.asbointl.org or call (703) 708-7069.

# CHAPTER 1

# School Bus Tracking and Safety
## Transportation

Brian P. Loncar
Supervisor of Transportation
Wilson School District
West Lawn, PA

*CCD District Details: 10 schools; 4,998 students; "urban fringe"; 701 total staff; 411 "other staff"; total 2001–2002 expenditures: $49 million*

School bus rider safety and coordination have always presented transportation managers and school administrators with an array of challenges and responsibilities. A recent incident in Berks County brought these issues unexpectedly to the forefront. What started out as a normal ride to school for 13 students in Berks County, Pennsylvania, quickly became a terrifying parental ordeal when a bus was hijacked and was missing for more than six hours.

It was not until after attendance was taken that school administrators realized that one of their buses had not arrived on schedule and was missing. Almost an hour after the students' scheduled arrival, unsuccessful attempts were made to contact the bus via radio, mobilizing administrators and authorities into action. The search quickly became far-reaching as authorities in neighboring states became involved in the search. Finally, after six hours of searching, the bus was located over 150 miles away in the state of Maryland.

Fortunately the children were returned safely, but the frustrating and helpless feelings during the incident left their mark on school administrators, parents, and students. It underscored the need to search for solutions that would provide tools to aid school administrators and authorities should such an event occur in their district.

This incident served to confirm to Wilson School District the foresight it displayed over two years ago. At that time Joe Winkler, a former Wilson graduate, contacted Wilson's Superintendent, Dr. Lee Fredericks, about an idea for a school bus notification system. Dr. Fredericks then called together as members of a team the Supervisor of Transportation and the Director of Finance and Support Service, who in conjunction with the Superintendent evaluated the proposed concept and the viability of its use in Wilson School District's transportation plan.

When Joe contacted Wilson, he had nothing more than an idea. As initially conceived, the *Here Comes the Bus* system notifies households through a wireless pager of the number of minutes and miles their child's bus is from their bus stop. As Wilson officials and Joe worked together, the concept was broadened to capitalize upon the capabilities of Global Positioning System (GPS) technology.

What resulted from this cooperative interaction was a GPS tracking system that provides notification to households, in addition to providing to the District, such vital information as realtime maps of all school bus locations and speeds, down to the street level. The tracking system also provides automatic alarms if a bus is stopped in an unauthorized zone or diverges from its normal route beyond preset parameters. This information allows buses to be monitored more closely, enhances overall bus safety, and provides a tool to parents who wish to avail themselves of the service offered by the system. We at Wilson are proud to have assisted in the development of the *Here Comes the Bus* School Bus Tracking and Notification System—a valuable tool for both the school and its community.

In the hijacking incident previously mentioned, the *Here Comes the Bus GPS* tracking system would have provided Wilson with an automatic alarm when the bus strayed off course. After receiving the alarm, the bus location could have been quickly identified. We believe this system would have provided the District with information that could have assisted authorities to more quickly locate the missing bus. Before this incident occurred, the District was also investigating rooftop identification as an additional tool to locate any vehicles. The District believes that the safety of its students demands constant monitoring and careful evaluation of any methods and/or technologies to help protect its students.

Since Wilson served as a pilot district assisting in the development of the *Here Comes the Bus* system produced by Joe Winkler's company, Everyday Wireless LLC, Wilson received all of the technology at no cost. Dr. Fredericks, Lorraine DeTurk, and I assisted Joe and Everyday Wireless in securing school board approval on October 17, 2001 to deploy the system as soon as the technology was fully developed and tested. The decision was based on nothing more than the conviction that such a system would help to further school bus safety. Limited prototype field tests with Everyday Wireless were begun in May of 2000.

Wilson School District believes this technology has the potential to provide ancillary cost savings to our school and others. At the current time, school bus routing software has very limited capabilities, not because of software shortcomings, but because the software lacks the necessary real-world data to provide optimized inputs. Real-time tracking will quantify traffic patterns, driver tendencies, and route characteristics and could be the breakthrough for truly optimizing bus routing. In addition, it provides transportation supervisors with documentation to investigate and respond to queries concerning bus speeds, driver locations in emergencies should radio correspondence fail, etc.

As school administrators search for solutions to track their buses and optimize their routing, we believe, cooperative partnerships such as the one Wilson has developed with innovators like Everyday Wireless can only benefit schools and their communities, both in the present and in the future.

# CHAPTER 2

# Electronic Solution for Print Shop

## Technology, Internal Operations

Marilyn Marklevitz
Superintendent of Financial Services and Treasurer
Waterloo Regional District School Board
Kitchener, Ontario

*2001 School District Total Revenue: $380 million*

We are a large urban school board with 61,500 students in 100 elementary and 15 high schools. Our school district covers 530 square miles and we have an expenditure budget of $380 million. The school board has had a print shop in its education center since the formation of the board in 1969. The printing services provided to the board included a wide range of items, such as letterheads, school newsletters, reports, curriculum documents, student exams, workbooks, manuals, and school calendars. The shop employed three full-time employees and a supervisor. Much of the equipment including offset presses had been acquired in the wealthier funding days of the 1970s and 1980s. Since the early 1990s available capital funds have been severely reduced and the last major equipment upgrade was a large document reproduction machine purchased in the mid-1990s. The board's courier system was utilized to transport the master information to the central print facility and the finished product back to the schools.

In early 1999, an independent review of potential Y2K issues revealed that about $50,000 was needed to guarantee that the existing system would be operational on January 1, 2000. Another $100,000 would be needed to complete electronic connectivity centrally to all

115 sites so that print jobs could be submitted online. In two to four years a new investment of $500,000 would be required to keep pace with technological advances to the major piece of hardware. In addition, other equipment, although in working condition, was outdated, parts were scarce and expensive, and the operation was labor intensive. A further $100,000 would be required to adequately address the problems associated with the printing presses. To further complicate the issue, the school board's printing volume had been declining in the past few years thereby increasing the per unit fixed costs and driving internal costs upwards. Production volumes varied significantly during the year resulting in expensive overtime during peak periods or alternatively contracting out at market rates. At other times staff were virtually idle. Technical support could not be provided in-house and was expensive to purchase.

It was obvious that we needed a creative solution for our potential print shop "millennium bug." We issued a "request for information" to investigate methods to replace our print shop delivery mode. We looked at traditional supply methods where we would merely contract the work out and we also researched more innovative government supply options. Our eventual choice was to work in partnership with our local university graphic arts and print shop. The university was well known for its progressive approach to technology and had a modern shop, which ran 24 hours a day, and, fortunately for us, had excess capacity available. They were also experiencing difficulties finding and maintaining trained staff to operate their equipment.

They began a process of negotiation with the university. Time was of the essence because of the looming millennium issue. In the true spirit of cooperation, a solution was devised and we were up and running on January 1, 2000, offering a seamless transition of existing services and thus averting a potential crisis. The greater benefit for us was that we were also able to enhance our product offering and this was made available to schools in early 2000.

However, the major advantage for the school board was the ability to electronically send print jobs from each of our 116 sites (115 schools and the education center) to the university. This part of the arrangement was rolled out during 2000 as each site was contacted and trained by university personnel. This cut the turnaround time for print jobs in half and also improved the image reproduction quality. Greater efficiency was also achieved and time-consuming setup time reduced because their electronic archival system allows them to store templates for letterheads, etc. and print them on demand. The university also offers a wide range of additional services to our sites, including book binding, color printing, and separations, multiple forms printing, graphic design, custom publishing, electronic imaging, offset printing, scanning and archiving, reprographics, document processing, and document finishing.

Our new partner was also in a win-win situation. The university was able to improve its excess capacity situation and thereby support its capital equipment replacement program by covering its fixed costs. They were also able to acquire three highly qualified personnel from the school board. These individuals now have the advantage of a much larger print operation in which to upgrade their skills and knowledge. Their old equipment was utilized as back-up or replacement parts for the university's equipment. The additional paper volume also created the potential for the school board to share favorable paper pricing with the university due to a cooperative buying arrangement.

## COST ANALYSIS

Capital: The school board saved capital equipment replacement costs (five year projection) as shown in Table 2.1.

Operating: Annual operating costs of the print shop were $550,000.

**Table 2.1    Major Hardware Costs**

|  | Major Hardware Costs: |
|---|---|
| Year 2000 | $150,000 |
| Year 2002 to 2004 | $500,000 |
| Total | $650,000 |
| Upgrades to Other Equipment | $100,000 |
| Total | $750,000 |

This was recovered through charges to users. However, many costs, including technical support and training were predicted to increase significantly. The decreasing volume had driven per unit costing upward for individual print jobs.

The transition to the university print shop reduced operating costs in a number of ways. The 116 sites experienced a reduction in costs associated with print job setups on repeat orders. Individual pricing was adjusted to reflect more realistic costs and high volume print jobs were more favorably priced for all users.

In the future, it is expected that the volume purchasing for paper will further advantage the cooperative venture partners.

## EVALUATION

Advantages to the school board:

- Immediate avoidance of Y2K problem with equipment
- Longer term avoidance of replacement capital equipment costs
- Online Internet connectivity allowing electronic transmission of print jobs to all sites thereby reducing turnaround time and increasing print quality
- More graphic and print services and products available to school sites and offices
- Better pricing based on participation in shared volume level
- Avoidance of duplication of equipment and human resources
- Redeployment of staff who would otherwise have remained on the school board staff
- Provision of extra courier service for deliveries by the university
- Avoidance of future increasing service and training costs
- Telephone support desk for school board users
- Technical support for operations

Advantages to the university:

- More fully utilize machine capacity
- Back-up equipment and replacement parts acquired

- Access to better pricing, particularly on paper, based on combined volumes and existing arrangements
- Acquisition of experienced, trained staff
- Avoidance of duplication of equipment and human resources
- Added volume contributes to fixed equipment costs

## COMMUNICATION

The project was mostly an internal and transparent improvement to the efficiency of the print shop. Product catalogs and color and paper samples were distributed to each of the 116 sites. University staff visited all sites to establish the appropriate electronic links and to ensure a comfort level with the submission of print jobs. The practice has been noted as an example of cooperation in educational partnerships.

## SUMMARY

The seamless transition from an onsite, outdated print shop with limited capabilities to an electronic partnership with a community-based public sector educational partner has greatly benefited both parties. Both have achieved more effective costing of their services and avoided duplication of expensive capital equipment and human resources.

The lesson learned for all school boards is one of efficiency and non-duplication of resources. Operational cost efficiencies can be achieved through volume purchasing of raw materials and economies of scale associated with performance levels. Increasing service levels by optimizing product offering is another qualitative by-product of this project.

The consolidation and concentration of expensive capital resources at one site in order to serve multiple partners maximizes the utilization of the equipment and avoids the costly duplication of capital.

# CHAPTER 3

# Implementing Change in Facilities Management

## Facilities Management

John Chardavoyne
Assistant Superintendent
Stamford Public Schools
Stamford, CT

*CCD District Details: 22 schools; 15,053 students; "Mid-size central city"; 2,126 total staff; 883 "other staff"; total 2001–2002 expenditures: $159 million*

## OVERVIEW OF CHANGE

In July of 2000, a school district made the commitment to completely overhaul its facilities department. The entire philosophy and approach to facilities management would be changed from the top down, including the reorganization of central management and supervision, new budget controls, installing new preventative maintenance programs, and reallocating personnel throughout the school system. The District planned to reengineer the way in which it did business.

The commitment would be one of dedication and perseverance. The department was faced with a poorly trained and less than productive custodial staff, skyrocketing budget increases, an aging infrastructure with numerous fire code violations, and a complete lack of communication with the school community at large. Compounding these operational difficulties was the strained relationship between central office staff and the custodial union. At the beginning of July, the facilities

11

department had more than eighty (80) grievances and unfair labor charges pending with City and State arbitrators. The one factor effectively green-lighting a massive change effort: *It couldn't get worse, could it?*

The district understood that management of facilities was not one of its core competencies and viewed outsourcing as a necessity to execute the district's change effort. An outside facilities management organization was chosen as the district's partner to streamline existing business processes and to create a professional work environment for administrators, principals, and maintenance staff to excel in.

## PURPOSE OF CHANGE

The mission of the change program is to coordinate the physical workplace with the people and work of the organization. The district's new facilities management processes would integrate principles of business administration, architecture, and the behavioral and engineering sciences. In doing so, it could create a positive cascading effect on every aspect of the facilities enterprise. Personnel, administrative, and infrastructure segments were addressed concurrently over the next twenty-four months. The following is a brief account of some of the efforts.

### Team Leader Program

Without open and honest communications between management and staff, successful change programs, no matter how well thought out, are destined for failure. The district realized that only an approach that ensures cooperation from both parties would allow the system to move in a positive direction. With this belief the first system, called the *Team Leader* concept was installed. The Team Leader program takes qualified Head Custodians and/or Trades Foremen and elevates them to positions of management. In addition to their own school or trades staff, they serve as building liaisons for principals and other head custodians throughout the district.

The program benefits both management and existing custodial staff.

First, we have created additional upward mobility for our employees who, historically, were at the pinnacle of their careers. The Team Leader program provides a stipend, additional responsibility, and increased training opportunities. Second, Team Leaders serve a vital role in opening lines of communications among all district personnel. Similar to a *clerk-of-the-works* on a construction project, these individuals are the eyes and ears of the district. Complaint calls once placed directly to central office are now routed to the Team Leaders where they are addressed immediately. Finally, the assignment of four Team Leaders has served to create a working relationship with the custodial union that services the district first.

## Resource Allocation

Reallocating personnel from day shifts to night was an immediate goal of the department and as of March 4, 2002, each school in the district has a night shift in place. The addition of the night shift allows custodial staff to clean additional square footage due to the fact that the bulk of work is performed while the school is unoccupied. With no additional personnel, the district will have cleaner, more efficient schools at a reduced cost. Two test cases were implemented in the 2000–2001 school year and proved extremely successful. The schools have never looked better and the department saw average weekly overtime drop from twenty man-hours to four. This represents savings of roughly $30,000 per location that will be used for much needed preventative maintenance programs throughout the school system.

## Overtime Management

Prior to July 2000, the district's overtime costs were out of control. The challenge for the year was to cut the need for excessive overtime without sacrificing the service or effectiveness of the district's custodial staff. We have implemented the following management controls with amazing results:

- Strict guidelines as to what constitutes an overtime event. *(Note: this is an enforcement of the Union's collective bargaining agree-*

*ment that had never been performed. Over the past few years, overtime was seen as a natural extension to daily duties and abused often with no controls in place.)*

- Requests for overtime are now submitted in writing to the facilities department and must include a description of the event or activity, the number of personnel, and overtime hours necessary. The application is forwarded to both the building Principal and the Facilities Manager who approves, edits, or denies the request.
- Each Monday, Head Custodians submit a weekly report that itemizes overtime by individual and event. This information is entered into a database created by the district's management company and is used to generate reports that accurately accounts for and charges outside groups *(or construction projects)* for custodial overtime. The money is then credited back to the facilities budget.

Overtime management and enforcement is a full-time job for the facilities department. During the 2000–2001 fiscal year, the custodial staff of approximately 145 members worked in excess of $1.6 million in overtime. Maintaining precise controls to appropriately credit the facilities budget requires constant attention. The district continues to impose strict policies on how overtime is managed throughout the district in order to enforce its fiduciary responsibility.

**CMMS Application Project**

The district is in the process of developing a new Computerized Maintenance Management System *(CMMS)* that will offer the department the ability to centralize, automate, and manage plant operations online. This includes life safety equipment, computer inventory, and service contracts among many others. The district will be implementing a completely web-based work order system next fiscal year.

A note must be made regarding the CMMS product and its potential for the district. This application can and will be used by any enterprise responsible for maintaining facilities. However, the district is one of the first systems in the region taking advantage of Internet technologies and putting it to practical management use. The project, currently co-funded by the City's surplus school building use account, will produce a tool that will centralize all data, reduce costs and boost operating efficiency throughout the district and represents the culmination of all of our change efforts.

## COST ANALYSIS OF CHANGE

The District understands that change is an ongoing, ever-evolving process that will continue to be refined. However, the preliminary cost analysis of our efforts is simply astounding. The following is a brief demonstration of the results over the past eighteen months:

- City Recreation Overtime Reduction:    $100,000
  The city's Recreation department is the single largest community user of the school buildings. Overtime costs due to poor resource allocation were prohibiting the expansion of recreation programs.

- ROSCCO Overtime Reduction:    $75,000
  ROSCCO is an after-school program for the community's elementary-school-aged children. The program would have been forced to raise fees in order to pay for custodial overtime without some type of intervention.

- School Building Use Program:    $250,000 increased revenues
  This revenue, derived from accurate overtime charge-backs, is funding the continued development of the CMMS application project, which will in turn generate additional savings for the district.

- Night Shift Implementation:    $30,000 per location
  Up to $500,000 in savings is projected by year three of our change program, which will be used to fund much needed capital repairs and equipment in the years to come.

The positive implications of these results cannot be understated. Remember, these results were primarily achieved in the second year of the program. Year-over-year results will continue to generate additional savings as we see continued operational improvements from the system-wide implementation of our night shifts. This will allow us to increase our repair and equipment line items not normally carried in our operational budget and move on to the implementation of comprehensive preventative maintenance programs for both custodial and trades personnel.

## EVALUATION OF CHANGE

The district's change program and renewed philosophy of management has been an unqualified success. We were able to establish a professional work environment out of which the needs of students are always placed first. Buildings have never been cleaner. Overtime is manageable. To date, the district has yet to have one single grievance or unfair labor charge reach arbitration status. The $13 million facilities budget will remain flat from 2001–2002 to 2002–2003 for the first time in a number of years.

Costs are easy to spot as a program's benchmark for success. Indeed, in these economic times the district certainly takes its budgetary victories seriously. However, it is the collaborative spirit generated through our efforts among central office, custodial staff, building principals, and the community at large that remains our most remarkable achievement. As long as this dynamic remains intact, fiscal gains will continue to be made.

## COMMUNICATING CHANGE

The district's goal was to achieve measurable results and communicate them throughout the system. We first needed to establish a benchmark of the current situation that was recognized district-wide as a starting point for change. During the summer of 2000, personal interviews were conducted with key school community stakeholders (board officials, principals, administrative staff, custodial staff, etc.) who provided insight as to the perceived strengths and weaknesses of the department. We then provided tours for Board of Education and City officials of each school building so that decision makers had a keen understanding of the conditions we were working under. These individuals had both direct and indirect input in the development of each system. Each new system or program implemented was performed only after it was communicated with each stakeholder. It is our opinion that success could not be achieved any other way.

The success of this model is evidenced by the fact that the municipality in which the school district resides has outsourced its facilities operations to the same firm.

# CHAPTER 4

# Creating a District-Wide Energy Management Program

## Energy Efficiency, Transportation

Robert W. Dooley
Director of Business Affairs
Warwick Public Schools
Warwick, RI

*CCD District Details: 27 schools; 12,222 students; "Mid-size central city"; 1,478 total staff; 556 "other staff"; total 2001–2002 expenditures: $113 million*

In September 1999, in my role as Business Manager for a school district with 12,000 students and 30 school buildings, I initiated a multi-faceted energy management program with the goal of reducing energy consumption, saving money, and reducing our reliance on nonrenewable energy resources while at the same time improving overall building comfort and remaining environmentally friendly. Since this was such a large task to tackle, we have phased in a number of initiatives over the last two years and we are researching and testing additional concepts to add to our program. We view this program as one that will continually evolve and expand as new technology advances become identified.

The first step was to hire an Energy Manager who would report directly to me as Business Manager and work exclusively on energy related projects and issues. Our first two goals were to study our fuel purchasing procedures to see if we could identify ways that we could reduce costs by more effective energy purchasing policies and to build a consumption-data baseline for the prior year using a computerized energy management system for accountability. As a result of this purchasing review, the district has initiated the following product procurement procedures that have significantly lowered the unit costs for the various products that we use:

**Heating oil fixtures.** In the spring of both 2000 and 2001 we purchased heating oil futures for the following winter that locked our per gallon prices for the next heating season. This not only lowered our costs considerably but it also made it much easier to build and monitor our budget for that fiscal year. We are about to repeat this initiative by buying oil futures now for the 2002–2003 winter.

**Natural Gas.** In the fall of 1999 we entered into a cooperative purchasing agreement with our state purchasing department to purchase natural gas at the state unit price, which was well below the price we were able to obtain on our own. We were the only school district in the state to initiate this cooperative purchasing with the state. Their three-year contract will expire on November 1, 2002, and we are already working with the state to participate with them in a new cooperative purchasing contract when that one expires.

**Electricity.** We joined an electricity purchasing pool coordinated by our state's association of school committees prior to the hiring of our energy manager. This cooperative purchasing project was started in 1997 but our Energy Manager was able to study our bills and the prices that were being charged under this agreement and found a number of overcharges that resulted in rebate checks to us in the amount of $286,000 over the last eighteen months.

In addition to saving money on our product procurement, I have worked with our Energy Manager to obtain a number of energy management grants through the national Rebuild America/Energy Smart Schools program as well as various grants from our state's Department of Energy. Examples of grants that have already been awarded are as follows:

**Lighting.** Over the last year we have received $180,000 in utility grant funding for energy efficient lighting in our schools. Some of this funding was for lighting in new building additions and some of the funding was for retrofitting some existing buildings with more energy efficient lighting. When the state legislature passed a bill authorizing the continuance of these state grants this year, I was invited to the Governor's signing of the bill to recognize our significant participation in the program.

**Solar Energy.** We received a $46,000 grant to install a photovoltaic roof system at one of our high schools. This will cover over 90 percent of the cost of the project and we will contribute the other $4,000 required to install the system. This system will be used to save money but also as an educational tool by the school. The electricity generated by the system will power student projects such as a weather station, an electric car, and several of our technology classrooms and will also produce enough electricity to sell back to the electric company. While we expect to recoup our $4,000 investment in a relatively short period of time, our primary goal was to utilize this project as an interdisciplinary tool to teach students the importance of renewable energy resources.

**Biodiesel Fuel.** We were the first school district in the country to receive a grant to purchase biodiesel fuel for space heating. This enabled us to save a little money but mostly allowed us to test and study this new fuel concept in our schools. We believe biodiesel fuels and possibly other renewable energy sources will become a significant part of the future for all energy consumers. We have already been awarded a grant in the amount of $10,000 for space heating and another $6,000 for transportation fuel as part of Phase 2 of our state's Department of Energy biodiesel program.

By having the Energy Manager report directly to me, he is free from being tied up with various maintenance issues and can devote all of his time to energy related issues. As a result, our Energy Manager has initiated an Energy/Construction subcommittee composed of himself, our construction coordinator, and some senior maintenance staff. This committee reviews all of our construction/renovation plans to ensure that all such projects are being designed and built in the most energy efficient way while still maintaining appropriate building comfort and utility. Since we received a $26.5 million dollar bond authorization by our taxpayers in 2000 to build additions and to renovate all of our school buildings, this committee has been invaluable in working with our architects, engineers, and contractors to maximize energy efficiency in all of our school construction projects. Over the last two years, we have added a total of approximately 100,000 square feet as school additions to various school buildings.

In addition, this committee has been active in analyzing all of our buildings and recommending a number of energy savings concepts that required a capital investment. For example, we have installed new control systems in some of our buildings, replaced steam traps, installed timer-controlled energy efficient outdoor lighting, installed new weather insulated doors, purchased energy management boiler control systems, increased insulation, etc. These measures have lowered our energy consumption and costs while also creating a more stable building climate and better learning environment.

I have met regularly with our Director of Buildings and Grounds, the Energy Manager, and various maintenance department tradesmen to make sure that we were all on the same energy-savings page. With input from our staff and supervision from our Energy Manager, working as a team, we have been able to institute a number of concepts that require no investment but still achieved significant results. We have reduced steam and water temperatures in our boilers, reduced boiler run times, instructed staff to turn off lights when areas are not in use, and initiated strict shutdown procedures and team-cleaning concepts for weekend and holiday periods. We have contracted with Energy Education Inc., a private consultant, to assist us with this consumption reduction portion of our overall program.

Our Energy Manager has worked with our teaching staff, especially math and science, to provide information and support for our curriculum as evidenced by our high school photovoltaic project. We are also studying new concepts to incorporate into our overall energy management program. We are currently studying on-site cogeneration of energy resources as well as the use of waterless toilets and the expansion of our biodiesel program for fuel for our maintenance vehicles and school buses.

In summary, I believe that we have instituted a very effective district-wide energy management system that is certainly unique to our state and could serve as a model for other school districts. We have incorporated creative purchasing concepts, utilization of available grant funding, a reduction of energy consumption, and improved energy efficient construction philosophies to create a better educational environment for our students and staff. We have incorporated a program that has reduced our energy costs significantly, resulting in a decrease in our heat and electricity budgets by approximately 25 percent, resulting in a cost avoidance of approximately $1,000,000 over the last two years. And while creating such savings, we have been able to make our buildings more comfortable and consistent resulting in fewer complaints about buildings that are too cold or too warm. Our program shows our concern for the environment by using and studying the use of renewable energy sources and has our entire district on board with an energy conservation philosophy. Our School Committee has endorsed our program and we have given two progress reports to the committee in public meetings to inform our community of our program and our efforts.

# CHAPTER 5

# Human Resources Department Web Access

## Technology, Human Resources Management

Frederick W. Gardiner
Manager, Benefits and Payroll
Dufferin-Peel Catholic District School Board
Mississauga, ON

*2001 School District Total Revenue: $575 million*

## OVERVIEW

With the current shortage of qualified teachers and other professionals, school boards are competing to attract new employees and retain current ones. To accomplish this, many school boards are looking for cost-effective ways to provide additional services for their employees.

The Dufferin-Peel Catholic District School Board launched an employee web access program in April 2001. They were looking for more efficient ways of delivering information to employees and decided to use the web as their primary communication tool.

The Human Resources Web Access system has been operating for a year. We have continuously added features as needs have been identified. What started out as a website to deliver employee information has quickly become an administrator's aide for hiring, leave, absence, as well as supplying teacher and accounting information.

We have been working on a document management plan since 1995. Our Board staff has grown by 1,300 employees since 1995 while the human resources staff has shrunk by five employees (10 percent). We simply needed to create efficiencies in our document distribution.

## PURPOSE

* The efficient delivery of employee demographic information. We expect to save two staff members if 50 percent of our employees sign up for web access. We currently deliver 8,400 pay statements to 200 sites 26 times a year.
* The timely delivery of staffing information to administrators. In March of 2001 we held focus group meetings with school Principals and Vice-Principals and asked them to tell us how to serve them better.

## COST ANALYSIS

The savings of two staff members in payroll and benefits plus distribution costs is expected to save $100,000. The development of the technical setup was done with existing software and hardware so no new cost was generated. The support and implementation of the project was provided by existing human resources and information technology staff.

## COMMUNICATIONS

Primarily we communicated the new system by e-mail to employees. For administrators I spoke at a Principal and Vice-Principal meeting and gave a brief demonstration. We provided information in a quarterly benefits newsletter, the *Director's Bulletin*, and ran a contest co-sponsored by our benefits provider. In the coming year we will speak at a school staff meeting (in our pilot we found that 80 percent of teachers at a school signed up after a 15-minute demonstration). Table 5.1 shows employee web access participation.

Employees may sign up by sending an e-mail requesting the service. We respond with a username and password, which must be changed the first time they log in.

**Pay statements.** Available from January 1, 2001, to date, we expect

**Table 5.1   Employee Web Access Participation, April 28, 2002**

| Employee Group | Web Access | Active employees | Percent | No Access |
|---|---|---|---|---|
| CUPE 2026 ten month | 197 | 343 | 57.4% | 146 |
| CUPE 2026 twelve month | 95 | 98 | 96.9% | 3 |
| Elementary Teachers | 445 | 2,830 | 15.7% | 2,385 |
| Elementary Principals | 111 | 113 | 98.2% | 2 |
| Secondary Principals | 23 | 23 | 100.0% | |
| Secondary Teachers | 295 | 1,620 | 18.2% | 1,325 |
| Elementary Vice-Principals | 70 | 77 | 90.9% | 7 |
| Secondary Vice-Principals | 51 | 54 | 94.4% | 3 |
| Letters of Permission—E | 3 | 83 | 3.6% | 80 |
| Letters of Permission—S | 1 | 53 | 1.9% | 52 |
| Assigned Occasional—E | 6 | 112 | 5.4% | 106 |
| Assigned Occasional—S | 6 | 63 | 9.5% | 57 |
| APSSP | 45 | 171 | 26.3% | 126 |
| Certified Supply | 2 | | | |
| Continuing Education | 5 | | | |
| CUPE 1483 | 53 | 573 | 9.2% | 520 |
| ERW | 59 | 404 | 14.6% | 345 |
| Mid Management | 114 | 119 | 95.8% | 5 |
| Senior APSSP | 2 | 3 | 66.7% | 1 |
| Supervisory Officers | 15 | 15 | 100.0% | |
| Temporary Employees | 47 | | | |
| Trustees | 1 | 11 | 9.1% | 10 |
| Lunchroom Supervisors | | | | |
| Emergency Instructors | 7 | | | |
| Chaplains | 2 | 6 | 33.3% | 4 |
| **Total** | **1,658** | **6,771** | **24.5%** | **5,177** |

to be able to maintain at least two years, we plan to notify web users when we start purging and/or archiving old statements. Employees can copy their statement to their hard drive and or print their pay statements on their local printer.

**Benefit profiles.** These include current employee demographic data, annual salary and allowances, benefit enrolment (including links to benefit coverage descriptions and forms), TD 1 information, and pension enrollment.

**Absence statement.** Online statement of current year absences and balances for sick and vacation credits as well as absences for Board related business. Employees are notified 14 days prior to data being purged. This data is duplicated for designated administrators.

**Seniority/Qualification.** For teachers and education resource workers only seniority data at the Board and by panel is displayed plus a summary of an employee's qualifications. This data is duplicated for designated administrators.

## ADMINISTRATOR WEB ACCESS

**Staff List for Administrators**. This gives Principals and Vice-Principals the ability to list/view/sort data related to all staff at their particular location. Some of the data is date sensitive, meaning that if a certain date is entered the data will be listed according to that point in time. We have attempted to design each page in the web access system with general functionality:

- The data is columnar so that it may be easily copied to a spreadsheet
- Clicking on a column heading will sort the data either ascending or descending
- A timer has been set to "time-out" if the workstation is left for a period of twenty minutes or longer
- Columns that are highlighted in blue have "drill down features" meaning that if you click on the blue highlighted data further data will be listed
- For security reasons access to the above function is restricted to Principals and Vice-Principals by location and senior administrators at the Board.

Each of the functions is accessed using a button:

**Salaried.** A date may be selected for a staff list at a location. The screen provides count and FTE by employee group.

**Leaves.** List current and future leaves for staff at a location.

**Seniority/Qualifications.** List seniority data for all academic staff and educational resource workers. Seniority data is selected by choosing an employee group from a drop down menu.

Seniority Date      date placement on probationary status
Seniority Years     continuous seniority

| Board Years | total experience (including supply/short terms/etc.) |
| ELEM Years | total elementary experience |
| SEC Years | total secondary experience |
| Total Years | an individual's total experience |
| QECO | QECO Rating |

**Absences.** Lists absences and replacements by location code. A drill down menu is provided to access absences per individual and replacement payment detail.

**Timesheet.** List of timesheet staff attached to a location.

**Hire Pool/Prefer Pool.** The Hiring features allow administrators to view the new hires that have been hired for September 1, 2002, and occasional teachers that are available for short terms. (This replaced supply and new teacher lists provided four to five times a year that were outdated by the time they reached the school.) The ability to access the new hire pool, OECTA-OT's, and Uncertified Supplies means that the data is up to date at any point in time. Principals and Vice-Principals may access the lists along with the ability to review the qualifications and experience of available Occasional Teachers, make comments, and reserve staff for their school. Only new teachers currently not placed will appear. The Preferred Pool contains occasional teacher candidates that have been preselected for hire if the permanent teacher hire pool is not large enough. This feature provides the ability to reserve new teachers to provide time for interviewing, etc. When an administrator reserves a teacher, this will mean that this applicant will not be displayed to another administrator for 24 hours. Once the time has expired, then the employee will reappear for consideration by all. To reserve employees, administrators choose their location from the pull down menu under "Reservation Loc" and press the "Reserve staff on this page" button to activate the reservation. The comment column allows administrators to choose certain reasons why a new hire is not available for certain divisions or an opportunity to comment on the interaction that they have had.

**Jobs.** Lists the posted jobs from the JOBS Line, along with the candidates who have applied.

## ACCOUNTING INFORMATION

The accounting information page has been developed to allow schools and departments to track expenditures that have been paid through payroll. In 2001–2002 we introduced school-based expenditures for supply teachers. This function allows school administrators access to details of who was paid for the school year (year-to-date), by the month (ties to expenditure reports provided by Finance), and by pay date. The period is selected from the drop down menu. The account code is selected from the GL Account Code drop down menu. The accounting detail page displays the total dollars paid by employee. By clicking on the employee ID in the detail the dates paid for the individual employee are displayed. The absent page details the absent teacher data. This feature has been developed outside of the staff list for administrator function so school budget secretaries can access it.

## FUTURE DEVELOPMENT

Future plans include the following:

- Feature to allow administrators to select available Occasional Teachers by subject area
- Staff list to capture enrollments that will meet the needs of Planning, Human Resources, and Family of Schools
- Provide a Link to the Ontario College of Teachers
- Interactive information updates
- IPPS through SRB
- CLARICA interface
- Teachers Pension Plan interface
- OMERS interface

# CHAPTER 6

# Purchasing Department Website

## Technology, Purchasing

Wilma A. Gibbs-Matthews
Purchasing Agent
Fulton County Schools
College Park, GA

*CCD District Details: 77 schools; 69,841 students; "Urban fringe of large city"; 9,209 total staff; 4,570 "other staff"; total 2001–2002 expenditures: $545 million*

## OVERVIEW

We designed and implemented a government-to-business solution website for a school district purchasing department, which provides exposure to more vendors/contractors than a local database of vendors could possibly make available. The site is a proactive means of increasing competition, increasing purchasing efficiency, and making the purchasing process user friendly for both the customers and the vendors. Used as a tool to conduct purchasing business, the site has saved the school system more than $100,000 annually.

Not only was the establishment of a website for the Purchasing Department a unique and innovative idea, it was the first for a school district in the state. The web was searched to determine how many (if any) public school systems had a purchasing department with a separate website from the school system site. A separate purchasing department site is extremely important because a vendor looking for new business opportunities could easily get bogged down by a school system website. Research during the spring and fall of 1999 revealed that no other school system purchasing department in the state had a website that would allow a link directly to that site without first linking to the school system's main website. In fact, no school system in the United States could be found with such a site.

## PURPOSE

The purpose of our Purchasing Department Website is to provide wider vendor competition, better communication with customers (employees), and big savings for the school system. The site was designed to be a working tool to provide information via the Internet to prospective and existing vendors, as well as providing need-to-know information to customers via the intranet. The Internet site allows vendors to register online, provides information on how to do business with this organization, enables viewing of open solicitations that may be downloaded, and provides a direct 24 hours/7days a week e-mail link to buyers with questions.

In the past, to get registered to do business with this organization, vendors would complete a vendor application form (three pages, mailed from this Department to the vendor), mail it back to our Department where someone would enter the information into a database. Now if a vendor wants to be added to our vendor file, he/she can simply click onto our site, enter the information on the electronic form, and click the submit button. The application is received electronically and the vendor file is automatically updated. This process would have taken several days or even weeks in the past, but now the process only take a few minutes.

Vendors/contractors searching for new business opportunities no longer need to call this office and spend 20–30 minutes listening to someone explain to them what products are currently being solicited through bids or proposals. The website has a complete listing of all open solicitations. The vendors simply click the "solicitations" button. This part of the site provides a complete list of all open solicitations and addenda. The information provided is a quick summary of all business opportunities available at any time. The solicitation portion of the site provides the title of the project or the item being solicited, the name of the user's department, and the buyer assigned to administer and award the contract. The vendor may either download the document to his computer or print a copy of the document. If a vendor would like to e-mail questions to the buyer the site also provides this opportunity. Contacting a buyer is a very simple task when using our website; simply clicking on staff and then clicking on the e-mail icon beside the buyer name will accomplish this task. This portion of the site has decreased the number of calls to our buyers by over 75 percent. The e-mail also provides a personal touch because the vendor/contractors go directly to the buyers without having to go through a third person or being switched to voice mail. Buyers answer all e-mail within 24 hours of receipt.

Previously, paper copies of all solicitations were mailed to our vendors. We averaged approximately 120 solicitations a year consisting of about 40 pages each. Solicitations were sent to an average of 50 vendors. This added up to approximately 240,000 pieces of paper being mailed annually. That's 48 boxes of paper and how many trees? Now that solicitations and addenda are posted on the site, vendors receive a postcard alerting them to check the website for the new solicitation. Vendors then print out the forms and send their response by mail or similar means to the Purchasing Department. In the very near future, responses to solicitations, as well as awarding contracts electronically will be performed via the Internet.

## COST ANALYSIS

The vendor and catalog page on our website provides direct links to vendors under contract with our school system. Online ordering from this website became a reality in July 2000. Customers access the screen of contract-negotiated vendors from our site and enter orders via the Internet; thus saving money for the vendor by minimizing the human element. This basic premise of e-commerce allows vendors to pass these savings on to the school system. Presently, the following eleven vendors are online; Office Depot, Grainger, Dell Computer, Apple Computer, Follett, Carolina Biological, School Specialty, Brodhead Garrett, Sax Arts and Crafts, ABC School Supply, and W. T. Cox. This portion of the website is expected to provide a savings in excess of $80,000 this school year. Savings come from reduced prices negotiated specifically for website ordering. This portion of the website is also password protected.

A savings in excess of $20,000 a year in labor and materials has been accomplished by eliminating the cumbersome task of mailing paper solicitation packets and addenda to vendors. Now that solicitations and addenda are posted on the site, vendors receive a postcard alerting them to check the website for the new solicitation. Vendors then print out the forms and send their response by mail or similar means to the Purchasing Department. In the very near future responses to solicitations and awarding contracts electronically will be performed via the Internet.

The total estimated savings for this site is in excess of $100,000 annually.


## EVALUATION

The basics of our business have not changed with the start-up of our website but the communication of our business has. Communicating electronically with both customers and vendors has saved time and money. The website has been a tremendous success for this system, having over 22,000 hits in less than a year. The site has provided exposure of our requirements to new vendors who, in the past, would have never considered doing business with a school system. Competition has increased by 100 percent for some items. The increased competition serves to drive prices down or at least minimize cost and improve the quality of products.

Furthermore, it has decreased the number of telephone calls from vendors requesting information by over 90 percent. Vendors and customers now have a source of information which can be accessed anywhere and at anytime they need it.

## MARKETING THE SITE

The marketing of the site was a challenge. Announcements were mailed to all vendors in the vendor database. The postcards announced the site and requested that all existing vendors visit the site for all new and upcoming solicitations. E-mails were sent to all school system employees announcing the site with a direct link on the e-mail. We also advertised in local newspapers for a month. A unique marketing opportunity and great exposure for the site was provided by the magazine entitled *Government Procurement*, The Journal of Purchasing Professionals after a reporter discovered our site while doing research for an upcoming article. The article was published in the June edition of the magazine. The reporter was simply surfing the net and discovered the website. She was very impressed that a school system had taken the initiative and was doing a B2B e-commerce type of function. The article was a great means of marketing the site across the nation.

## CONCLUSION

The Internet portion of our website has allowed us to truly move into the twenty-first century and offers a totally new way of doing business. This procedure aligns the Purchasing Department with e-commerce methods used by some of our largest vendors such as Office Depot, Dell Computer, and Grainger Industrial Supplies. Possibly the most valuable element of our site is the posting of solicitations. Vendors may download to a file or print the solicitations at their location. Our communication of a solicitation addendum has gone from three to five days to immediate posting on the web. Time and the cost of doing business for our Department has been drastically reduced and support to our customers enhanced. The Purchasing Department website is well on its' way to becoming a model for other local government entities to emulate. In a very short time, it has established itself in a technological arena with an effectiveness and efficiency that is truly remarkable.

# CHAPTER 7

# Emergency Preparedness/Response CD ROM
## Technology, Safety

Guy M. Grace Jr.
Manager of Security
Littleton Public Schools
Littleton, CO

*CCD District Details: 27 schools; 16,590 students; "Urban fringe of large city"; 1,820 total staff; 893 "other staff"; total 2001– 2002 expenditures: $107 million*

## SUMMARY

School safety and the ability to respond to an emergency or crisis situation has never been more paramount to school administration. Emergency planning and safety is a necessary component in providing an environment that is conducive to learning/teaching. Students and teachers alike should be confident that district administration has taken precautionary steps toward emergency preparedness.

## OBJECTIVE

To that end, in the summer of 1998 the district Security Manager and Security Facilitator, supported by the Assistant Superintendent, Director of Property Management Services, and Supervisor of Building Operations embarked upon the tedious task of compiling site-specific critical information throughout the district. The objective was to assemble all data applicable to each site in one easily accessible format.

Technology provided the most efficient medium of data manipulation, storage, and retrieval via the computer and the compact diskette. Detailed data is compiled in a format that provides easy access to intimate knowledge of every facility/site in the district. Interactive maps enable area-specific navigation with links to audio and video support. A compact diskette was developed for each school and auxiliary site in the district.

## CONTENT

Each diskette provides a virtual tour of the entire facility. The user-friendly diskette contains comprehensive, interactive, hyper-linked data inclusive of, but not limited to, the following information:

- Emergency contacts: district level administration, site level administration, law enforcement, fire and rescue
- Main utility shut-off locations: electric, gas, water
- Security system device locations: access/secure panels and motion detectors
- Fire system device locations: enunciator panels, smoke detectors, pull-stations, sprinklers
- 3-D building floor plans: scaled floor plans depicting all rooms, walls, doors, closets, ingress/egress, etc. locations
- 3-D interactive maps: all rooms, halls, and site-specific locations are hyperlinked to photographs, video, and/or audio descriptions and information associated with the area selected
- Motion video, interior: video photography of all offices, rooms, hallways, closets, etc.
- Motion video, exterior: video photography of building exteriors, roofs, courtyards, parking lots, playgrounds, etc.
- Motion video, community-streets and adjacent neighborhoods within a three-block radius
- Aerial photographs: scaled aerial photographs of each *site*.

## ENDORSEMENTS

Initial demonstration to district administration and the Board of Education yielded a hearty endorsement for the project and authorization to broaden the scope and utilization to include intergovernmental agencies. City and county emergency response vehicles in local jurisdictions are equipped with computers enabling immediate on-site information access. The local law enforcement agency honored the district by endorsing the program as the standard for emergency preparedness/response planning.

Law enforcement representatives from 20 jurisdictions statewide joined together for a review of the program. The ensuing discussion centered on the need to implement the program in multiple arenas. Since that time, numerous city and county government agencies, school districts, and shopping malls in the state and two out-of-state entities have requested program initiation and implementation information from the district.

## RESOURCE REQUIREMENTS

**Hardware.** Development and implementation of this program is easily phased. Standard office computers equipped to run the equivalent of Office 98 and Internet Explorer 4.0 or above are sufficient to begin the process of data collection and manipulation. Assuming that the computer is already available, a writeable compact disk drive, digital camera, video camera, and flatbed scanner are required to sufficiently implement the program from a centralized location. The required equipment and supporting software could be purchased for approximately $3,000. Aerial photographs and three-dimensional floor plans are discretionary and can be obtained through purchased services and/or computer-aided design programs. Additional monies would be required for aerial photographs and three-dimensional floor plans or computer-aided drafting software.

**Employee.** The largest commitment required to produce an effective program is one of employee allocation. Approximately 140 hours dedicated to a 50,000 square foot facility should yield a comprehensive product. The majority of time allocated to the project will be consumed by computer-based data assembly and manipulation. Assembly and manipulation will require 85 percent of the employee resource allocation, the remaining 15 percent will be devoted to fieldwork compiling raw information.

Since inception in the fall of 1998, approximately 6,000 hours of planning, research, development, and promotion have been dedicated to the project. Additional undesignated components will be added to the program as technology advances and new uses arise.

## CONCLUSION

Primarily, the project was designed to provide all foreseeable site and facility information required in the event of an emergency or crisis situation. The information is assembled in a concise, orderly fashion that provides immediate access to the most up-to-date information. Emergency response time will be shortened considerably due to law enforcement and/or district administrations ability to assess available options and make informed decisions based on readily available information.

Additional uses have evolved since initial implementation. The information is a valuable administrative resource for maintenance and grounds management, custodial personnel allocation, and capital improvement planning.

The program has been enthusiastically embraced by district and site-based administration as well as local emergency response agencies. School districts and emergency response agencies statewide have requested information and/or assistance with regard creating a similar program for their use. Intergovernmental cooperation and support is key to creating strong communities.

# CHAPTER 8

# School Construction Institute
## Facilities Management

Richard H. Weeks
Business Manager
Grafton Public Schools
Grafton, MA

*CCD District Details: 5 schools; 2,268 students; "Urban fringe of large city"; 273 total staff; 123 "other staff"; total 2001–2002 expenditures: $15 million*

The First Annual School Construction Institute was planned over a period of 22 months and was sponsored by Massachusetts Association of School Business Officials and held on October 19, 2000.

## OVERVIEW OF THE INSTITUTE

The Institute is an annual, nonpartisan educational program for school and town officials and facility planners, pertaining to all aspects of new school construction and renovations. The purpose of the event is to give a "crash course" in school construction issues to members of my affiliate and to invited attendees. Workshops include project planning, legal affairs, designing for technology, security, design for early childhood education, and renovating old schools.

In December 1998, I organized a fifteen-member committee from my local affiliate and began organizing this event. The committee reviewed the work of dozens of our region's architects, construction attorneys and others prior to inviting eight lead presenters to participate. Those selected to present were experts in their fields.

Massachusetts has 1,899 public school buildings. Just as those throughout the country, many were constructed prior to World War II and are crumbling apart. Others were built for the baby-boom generation and need significant additions and renovations for increased enrollment and twenty-first century technology infrastructure. My state legislature expects to commit $4 billion in funding over the next decade to improve the situation. School and town officials and common citizens are not born with the innate knowledge and skills to plan and supervise the construction of a multimillion dollar school construction project. At my suggestion, my affiliate decided to find a solution to the professional development needed for public building committee members to prepare for the challenge ahead.

The Institute offers 5 one-hour sessions featuring eight different presentations. Each presentation is repeated several times so that everyone can attend sessions most relevant to him or her. What is unique about this Institute is that my affiliate wrote the syllabus for the workshops and worked with the lead presenters in building their presentations. In addition, there is an Architects' Showcase featuring the works of the region's top school designers. PDP certificates are awarded at each session.

The School Construction Institute is ideal for school building committee members and educators who would benefit from a "crash course" on school construction issues. Registration includes lunch and is about a third the cost of similar for-profit conferences.

## SUCCESS OF THE INSTITUTE

More than 320 school business officials, school building committee members, planners, architects, and vendors attended the First Annual School Construction Institute on October 19, 2000, at a local conference center.

Evaluation forms completed by attendees expressed pleasure with the workshop topics and presenters. While building the presentations, I was insistent that the presenters provide up-to-the-minute information, practical approaches and exchange of ideas, and case study opportunities. They are not permitted to promote specific goods or vendors' services. Approximately 25 minutes of each session is devoted to a formal presentation, followed by 25 minutes of questions and answers.

Approximately 24 vendors, designers, and architectural groups participated in the Architect's Showcase. Two vendors journeyed from Washington, D.C. A publisher of a magazine serving the industry flew in from California to attend and write an article for her newspaper. In gratitude to the presenters for participating, my affiliate gave them complimentary tables at the Architect's Showcase and waived registration and lunch fees.

In addition to the educational merits of the Institute, it became a wonderful team-building experience for my affiliate. Approximately 25 members served as moderators at the sessions, introducing the presenters and managing the question and answer sessions; or session monitors, managing the attendees and passing out Certificates of Attendance. Financially, this quickly became the second-highest annual income-producing event for my affiliate. Our Board of Directors plans to utilize this new income to expand other affiliation services for members.

## SCHOOL CONSTRUCTION INSTITUTE

In the United States, elementary and secondary enrollment is at a record 53.2 million, and is expected to reach 54.2 million by 2009. In addition to the existing schools in need of renovation and repairs, at least 2,400 *new* public schools will be needed by 2003 to accommodate rising enrollments and relieve overcrowding. (Source: U.S. Department of Education.)

Nearly every school business official's responsibilities include this traditional "bricks and mortar" function within our jobs. In recent years, it has been surpassed by attention to technology, school violence, and other hot-button issues. However, in future years we will be spending more time on school construction issues than on any other issues. Others could readily adopt the format that we established and sponsor similar school construction institutes. School business officials are perhaps better positioned to spearhead school construction institutes than most other school personnel or professional organizations.

# CHAPTER 9

# District-Wide Networked Connected Digital Copier Solution Integrated with a School-to-Career Program

## Technology, Internal Operations

Robert A. Berry
Business Administrator
Oyster River Cooperative School District
Durham, NH

*CCD District Details: 4 schools; 2,295 students; "Urban fringe of large city"; 303 total staff; 139 "other staff"; total 2001–2002 expenditures: $18 million*

After nearly a year of organizing and pitching a "connected copier" replacement program in a planned, on-going, and systematic manner, the school district implemented a district "WAN connected copier" solution. The solution included a school-to-career component that led to local funding support, community involvement, the establishment of a student-school-business collaboration, and almost total elimination of outsourcing of copy/print jobs.

In June 1999, the district partnered with a vendor to reach a fiscal solution to fund the installation of three network accessible "work horse" digital copiers to become the foundation of a multiyear copier replacement plan that would build upon a student school-to-career program providing work experiences for students. The vendor provided the expertise and training needed to utilize the "connectivity" of the copiers to end users in settings such as: classroom desktop computing, office computing, home computing, and building-to-building computing. District personnel, the school board, and the community provided the enthusiasm and support for a successful implementation.

I am pleased to report that the program has been implemented and once the kinks were ironed out, the faculty and students could not be happier. Copies can be printed two-sided, on three-hole punched paper, stapled, collated, and printed on varying paper/card stock. Student workers or district-employed staff distributes copy/print jobs to the four school sites, which are seven miles apart.

Still the question is asked: Why didn't we do this sooner? The answer is that we needed to assemble a dynamic group willing to put forth efforts researching the latest in technology tools, creation of providing centralized printed copy, taking a progressive approach to equipment replacement strategy that could provide a school-to-career experience through a curriculum, and a technology based environment. Until 1998 the right mix had not existed!

## PURPOSE

The purpose of this project was to construct and implement a plan utilizing limited resources to fund replacement of district-owned copiers. The charge was to develop a fiscal solution to replace an aging copier population and to meet the increasing requests of teachers and staff that wanted to avail themselves of new technology—networked digital copiers. Teachers and staff realized that there were many wasted hours standing at outdated copiers that did not collate, staple, or provide two-sided copies. Due to fiscal impacts, the district was looking for ways to reduce its cost for outsourcing of copy/print jobs and copier maintenance/supply contracts. At the same time the district was seeking opportunities to employ students in school-to-career activities. Therefore, the district sought a multipronged solution to a copier replacement problem.

## COST ANALYSIS

In addition to the district owning or leasing their copiers, the district incurred significant maintenance and supply costs. Costs for maintenance were increasing proportionate to the age of the equipment and the high volume usage. In past years, the district had expended considerable funds on the outsourcing of many jobs as a result of unreliable copiers unable to staple, collate, produce two-sided copies, or use various paper weights. It only made sense to research improving the copy/print operations of the district at less cost and more efficient use of staff time.

After finding a suitable vendor, the district was able to enter into a cost effective leasing program resulting in new "WAN connected" technology. The vendor provided equipment, training, support, and maintenance at approximately the same cost as existing maintenance agreements, supply budgets, and the cost of outsourcing copy/print jobs. The vendor is providing, at no cost, assistance with the district's school-to-career program (a valuable asset that would cost thousands to implement on it's own). The school-to-career program is providing work opportunities in a community that has very few opportunities for its youth to learn a trade.

## EVALUATION

The success of the implementation is best summed up by an e-mail I recently received from the school-to-career program manager, as summarized below:

- Usage has been by students and teachers alike
- School publications are being produced in-house, not out-sourced, such as: Advisee portfolios; Student Handbooks (all four schools); and Budget books
- Class use:
  - School History Calendar (school-to-career project)
  - The First Grade Calendar (school-to-career project)
  - Project World, an environmental magazine (students produced)
  - Tickets and brochures for student activities
- Teachers are printing directly from their classroom or home computers

- We wonder how we ever survived without it! The copies are phe-
nomenal! The usage has increased as teachers find creative ways
to make use of the capabilities such as booklet making, printing
front and back, and collating!

The value of the program cannot be expressed solely in terms of having met fiscal constraints. One must also evaluate on the basis of accep-
tance of the program and on that note I can state that the program is
successful! The idea, which started as an abstract concept of trying to
meet the usage demands of the district, the fiscal resources of the district, and requests of the educational community, is a success. The district is planning to expand the "connected copier" solution to replace
more of the aging copiers. A true testament to the integrity of the program!

This program could be implemented in any district, in any community. Successful implementations require an idea championed by dedicated staff and one that is approached in a planned, on-going, and
systematic manner. This program was successfully implemented
because of a commitment to work modification, staff and student devel-
opment/training, and a willing vendor.

## COMMUNICATION OF IDEA

In the summer of 1998, an innovative idea to provide the school district
with a cost effective and efficient means to fund copier replacement
was conceived. To couple this concept with a school-to-career program
was a dream to enhance opportunities for students. I met with the district leadership team to explain my conception of a "connected copier"
solution and how this solution could support their educational program
needs. The leadership representatives (principals, technology director,
superintendent, and special education director) responded favorably to
the idea, but had doubts about funding and implementation.

A committee of end users, including secretaries, librarians, tech support staff, students, and teachers, was formed to research the concept.
Once the research was complete, the committee requested the plan be

included in the district's budget. The superintendent did include the request in his final recommendation to the school board and the plan was brought forth to the Finance Committee of the school board, whose support was overwhelming. However, due to considerable fiscal pressure on the budget, the school board cut the plan, suggesting it be put off another year. The plan did not die. instead it took on a life of its own when members of the community requested that the district's budget committee reconsider the "connected copier" plan during it's review of the school board's budget proposal. The "connected copier" plan was presented and ultimately supported and championed by the budget committee. The school board then reconsidered the plan and included it in the final budget placed before voters in March 1999! In May of 1999, an RFP was prepared and three vendors responded. After very careful review, a vendor was selected to provide a "connected copier" solution. By late June and early July, contracts were signed, equipment was delivered, and district technology staff began training. It was not until the fall and winter of 1999 that the plan was fully underway.

My plan has been presented to others at state and local meetings. I have recently changed school districts and am holding meetings with the technology coordinators to seek their input into designing and implementing a similar plan. Communication of the implemented plan continues today!

# CHAPTER 10

# Design and Construction Database Linked to Photographic Documentation

## Technology, Facilities Management

Mark A. Shoop
Great Valley School District
Malvern, PA

*CCD District Details: 5 schools; 3,549 students; "Urban fringe of large city"; 440 total staff; 203 "other staff"; total 2001–2002 expenditures: $48 million*

Through the use of a standard database program and digital photography, we have developed a system in which we are able to review plans and specifications accurately and efficiently. During the review phase a digital structure is built inside the database that is linked to the actual photographs taken during construction. District personnel are now able to access quickly digital documentation and information about their buildings.

Experience has taught us that a construction project and the building it produces will only be as good as the blueprints and specifications that were used to construct the building. Since our desire was to obtain the highest level of quality in our project (two new schools and three complete renovations), we made a conscious decision to make the architects and engineers accountable. The problem we faced was, how could one person review and keep track of literally hundreds of blueprints and thousands of pages of written specifications in a timely fashion.

We also knew that inaccurate and hastily prepared "as-built" drawings are a poor source of information. They cannot be relied upon to reflect how the building was actually built. The questions we faced were: How could we inform someone 20 years from now what was installed under the concrete floor or inside that wall? How could we best preserve the knowledge and firsthand experience that the owner's representative gained during the design, review, and construction process?

During the design phase of our new middle school we identified two important needs that had to be addressed.

First we wanted an extremely accurate final record of our new middle school. This final record had to contain every intricate detail of the building just as it was constructed, because of the desire to access information about the systems and materials that were actually used to construct the building.

Second, we wanted to have easy access to those records. At any time, we want to easily access critical information about the building. We did not want to have to leaf through dozens and dozens of drawings or delve into any number of specification books that may or may not be accurate. We also needed to be able, at anytime in the future, to look behind any wall, above any ceiling, or beneath any floor to see what is actually there.

We have developed a very accurate record of our school building and the means to access the information easily. By combining standard computer programs and digital photography, we feel we have developed a very valuable tool. Our hope is that in the future when district employees need to know what's behind that wall, how many 400W metal halide fixtures light the gym, or what's the serial number of the Bell & Gosset chilled water pump in the boiler room, it's only a click away.

## BENEFITS TO THE SCHOOL DISTRICT

Benefits to the school district as a result of this database include the following:

- Very accurate plans and specifications: When we compare the number of "action items" recorded during plan review to the number that had been corrected by the time the project went to bid, it is obvious that the system was able to identify errors and omissions in the bid documents.

- A lower number of omission generated change orders. Fact: There have only been two change orders that have resulted from an omission in the contract documents. Our Middle School project is currently 95 percent complete.
- The construction process has been streamlined. Delays seem to be the norm in school construction, but the Middle School project in which we implemented this system is actually ahead of schedule.
- Lower bids. Actual bids were lower than projected costs. Square footage costs are lower than comparable projects in scope and quality.
- Accurate documentation. The system itself is the greatest measurable benefit for our school system. We have developed an accurate, easy to use tool for archiving and documenting conditions before, during, and after construction.
- Easy information retrieval. Rather than wading through piles and piles of blueprints in a basement storage room trying to find out what breaker shuts off the outlets on the west wall of Room 222, you simply open the database program on your computer and look at all the electrical devices in Room 222 and what circuits power them. This whole process has taken only seconds to retrieve the information you need!
- Uniqueness of the design is such that it easily makes the transition from the construction blueprint and specification review to a construction inspection tool, to a permanent record of the actual building as it was constructed through the use of digital photos.
- Use of the very latest technology. Personal computers can hold a wealth of data. Information needs to move from printed material (i.e., plans, specs, and submittals) to electronic media for review and archiving purposes. A simple database is used for this. Digital photographs are used for documentation and inspection, making those two processes much easier and faster.
- Groundbreaking approach to specification and blueprint preview. Architects and engineers are paid to produce a product. They

should be held to a high standard of accountability. Why should we settle for an incomplete, inaccurate product that could result in cost overruns during our building projects?

• This process puts school administration in control of the construction project by leading the district representatives through a detailed and systematic evaluation of the construction documents. During this process, it highlights inconsistencies and errors, thus forcing an early and cost-effective correction of errors and omissions.

• By following its systematic approach to data entry, it encourages the representative to find areas where value engineering can be applied.

## IMPLEMENTATION

The need is there: school districts have a responsibility to watch closely today's very expensive building projects.

Any school entity that is planning new construction or renovating an existing facility must decide how to administer their project. This can be done through a construction management company that takes an additional percentage of the project costs over and above the architect's fees, or through an employee of the school district. The use of a school district employee as the project representative is a far less expensive way to go. This system of construction document review and archiving gives the school district employee a high tech magnifying glass that he can use in the present and the future.

The technology is readily available. Most districts already have the software and hardware used in the system. Technology costs are dropping on a daily basis, making this an affordable investment. A personal computer, printer, and camera are all standard equipment for the Owner's Representative, so no additional cost were incurred to implement this system at our district.

School districts have the skilled personnel to implement this program. Most districts are currently teaching or using the two pieces of software used in the system. We currently are using Microsoft Access as the foundation of our system and PowerPoint for photographic display and documentation. Thus training and implementation costs are low.

# CHAPTER 11

# Redesign of Secondary School Reimbursable Meals Program: "Maxi-Meals"
## Food Service

Daniel J. Andrews
Director of Food Services
Seminole County Public Schools
Sanford, FL

*CCD District Details: 72 schools; 62,786 students; "Urban fringe of mid-size city"; 6,602 total staff; 3,208 "other staff"; total 2001–2002 expenditures: $374 million*

## OVERVIEW

The Seminole County Public Schools, a 52-school district, implemented the "Maxi-Meals" program, an unprecedented operational program that is increasing secondary-school student participation in the National School Lunch Program and thus reversing the national trend of declining participation. Utilizing Nutritional Menu Standard Planning, the district increased revenue, curbed costs, and offered secondary students industry-standard quality and presentation through this "Maxi-Meal" program.

## PURPOSES

The purposes of the program were:

- To ensure nutritional integrity through the NuMenu planning system while designing meals that resemble meals found in industry,

- To reverse the trend of secondary students not participating in the National School Lunch Program,
- To minimize purchased food costs, and
- To help educate students regarding proper portion sizes and balanced nutrition.

## COST/BENEFIT ANALYSIS

The cost of implementation of the "Maxi-Meals" program was approximately $2,000. This included:

- $200 in labor/benefits. Our Food Service Department's in-house Registered Dietician spent approximately four hours designing and nutritionally analyzing five initial "Maxi-Meal" menus.
- $1,800 in advertising. Printing flyers advertising the "Maxi-Meals" program to students, parents, and staff.

## EVALUATION/BENEFITS

At the high school level, from July 1, 1999, through March 2000, as compared to the prior school year, the Maxi-Meals:

- Increased revenue more than $140,000
- Increased total reimbursable meal sales at the high schools 44.9 percent and growing
- Increased "paid" reimbursable meal sales by 97.6 percent and growing
- Increased reimbursable meal participation by 3 percent
- Decreased purchased food cost by 3 percent
- Decreased labor for food preparation.

At the middle school level, from July 1, 1999, through March 2000, as compared to the prior school year, the Maxi-Meals:

- Increased revenue more than $400,000
- Increased total reimbursable meal sales by 32.9 percent and growing

- Increased "paid" reimbursable meal sales by 78.4 percent and growing
- Increased reimbursable meal participation by 3 percent
- Decreased purchased food cost by 3 percent
- Decreased labor for food preparation.

Overall, from July 1, 1999, through March 2000, as compared to the prior school year, the Maxi-Meals:

- Increased revenue more than $540,000
- Increased total reimbursable meal sales 37.7 percent
- Increased "paid" reimbursable meal sales 87.97 percent
- No change in a la carte sales volume.

## EVOLUTION OF THE PROGRAM

During the past ten years, there has been nationwide concern over decreasing lunch program participation at the secondary level. In order to maintain fiscally viable secondary programs, our district built an extremely aggressive a la carte program around the concept of providing our students with similar items as found in industry, at industry quality, and near industry pricing. However, while a la carte sales went up, reimbursable "paid" meal sales continued to decline yearly. *(Students of any age group will not eat foods that they are unfamiliar with or do not like. Cultural changes in family eating and dining out habits have significantly affected what foods are found acceptable in this age group.)* Our problems at the secondary level were declining reimbursable meal counts, increasing labor costs, and food cost control.

We isolated the production of the traditional reimbursable meal components as a potential problem with both food and labor cost. These food items were substantially different from the more marketable a la carte items. Also, we were assigning labor solely for their production and service. As the counts of reimbursable meals continued to decrease, the labor percentage and the amount of waste were becoming excessive. On the other hand, the items being sold through the a la carte program were culturally acceptable to the students. I made the decision to work within the students' culture to offer comparably appealing, reimbursable meals.

The commercial industry typically bundles products together in the form of sandwich, fries, and a drink combining separate items into "meals." Initially, I used this "bundle" concept for marketing our a la carte items. Realizing the marketability of the "bundles," I had our existing a la carte product bundles reformulated to create "Maxi-Meal" *reimbursable* bundles.

These "Maxi-Meals" (1) appealed to secondary students, (2) met USDA NuMenu guidelines for *reimbursable* meals, and (3) utilized products in our existing a la carte program.

The NuMenu guidelines allow districts to meet the nutritional requirements by weighting the nutritional analysis by numbers being served. This allows the offering of items that traditionally are thought of as "less nutritional" but are culturally desirable. By using items that we were producing as a la carte, we eliminated both labor and food waste.

Initially, five bundles (or "Maxi-Meals") were developed—each offering whole fruit, iced tea, and a choice of milk. The five "Maxi-Meal" entrees are:

- Hamburger/cheeseburger with lettuce, tomato with fries
- Pizza with fries
- Pasta (marinara or meat sauce) with a garlic breadstick
- Chicken nuggets with a roll and mashed potatoes (with or without gravy)
- Soup or salad with a garlic breadstick.

All "Maxi-Meals" are available on any line in our food courts, thus eliminating any stigma that may be attached to these meals. Also, I had the space used by the reimbursable lines in our food courts adjusted and created two lines for each of the formerly designated reimbursable lines. This gives us the ability to serve more students in a shorter period of time.

We used color-coding to help students recognize the "Maxi-Meals." In our brochures, on our menu boards, in our flyers, and on menus that we placed under Plexiglas on the serving lines, we color coded the "Maxi's" as yellow. This helped create product identification and promoted the ordering of these bundles. We then serve the minimum requirement for a reimbursable meal and have the other meal components offered at the point-of-sale. We also make sure that the minimum requirements that we serve are those items most desired by our customers. This minimizes waste and creates the greatest value in the minds of our customers.

After several months of familiarizing parents, staff, and students with these changes, we are now addressing more variety by designing "Maxi-Meals" that will be specials of the day/week. This not only allows us to provide more variety, but it addresses holiday meals and gives us the opportunity to identify bundles that have great appeal so that we can eventually replace slow selling "Maxi's" with ones that have more appeal.

The redesign of the reimbursable meal program for secondary schools is appropriate for any school district. In districts that have low free/reduced applications, the paying students are the largest market and the least saturated. In districts that have high free/reduced applications, the concern has to be customer satisfaction and the question is whether a program is providing for customer satisfaction when paying students do not see the value given and do not participate.

# CHAPTER 12

# Meeting Pupil Transportation Challenges through Cooperation and Innovation

## Transportation

Jonathan H. Ross
Director of Transportation
Southern Westchester Board of Cooperative
Educational Services (BOCES)
North White Plains, NY

*Note: CCD does not incorporate information for BOCES*

Throughout America school districts are striving to meet new challenges, and as they enter the new millennium it is very important that decisions made by all responsible parties in education reflect what is best *for the children.*

It has been said more than once, "The school day starts in the morning when children board their school bus and ends in the afternoon when they get off at their bus stop." How well a child does in school can be attributed to his or her school bus experience. During the current school year more than 24 million children ride nearly 450,000 yellow school buses to and from school each day. It is critical for every school board member, every school administrator, and every parent to realize that the school bus is an integral part of the child's school day. Simply stated, the time spent on a school bus is an extension of every rider's school day.

It is incumbent upon school business officials to make sure that the children of their school district be afforded safe transportation to and from school every day. It is equally important that this service be provided with a good measure of efficiency. During the 1990s school finances were under constant scrutiny and the fiscal realities of the times have had a harsh impact on school budgets. School districts have had to budget increasing amounts of money for pupil transportation services as their state transportation aid has been slashed dramatically. This shift in responsibility for providing the money to pay for these mandated services has moved from the state or local government to the taxpayer.

In response to the demanding times of tight fiscal policies, and higher parent expectations, four small suburban school districts with a combined enrollment of about 7,000 have resolved to work more closely with one another. In particular, these districts are sharing pupil transportation services to out-of-district schools and as a result have developed safer, more efficient programs for their children. This sharing of transportation services is occurring at unprecedented levels, and to assist with program administration the districts have retained the services of a regional educational consulting agency that serves the role of a "shared transportation manager." With the start of the 1999–2000 school year, the member school districts of this transportation consortium have managed to significantly reduce the number of bus routes they contract for, have a stable relationship with bus companies under contract, and are projecting a decrease in contract transportation costs of 25 percent.

## WHY JOIN A PUPIL TRANSPORTATION CONSORTIUM?

The development and subsequent implementation of this innovative transportation services consortium was primarily driven by the need to do what was best for the children who received transportation to schools outside their home district's boundaries. Although originally conceived in late 1997, it was not until the spring of 1999 that these four school districts decided it was time they all resolved to work cooperatively to provide school transportation for the 300 or so children who attended private, parochial, and special education schools. Under ordinary circumstances, transporting 300 children does not appear to be a difficult task. But when you begin to analyze exactly what services are provided and learn that these 300 children attend 85 different out-of-district schools all within approximately a 50-mile radius, the bigger picture comes into focus. Consider further that during the 1998–1999 school year these four school districts had a total of 55 school bus routes in place to transport their children. These 55 routes cost the districts $1.3 million or nearly $4,400 per student per year paid to private school bus companies.

The regional consulting agency is credited with developing the transportation consortium model and working diligently to see that the concept was sound enough to be attractive to the respective Boards of Education. The administrative teams of all four school districts were sold on the idea from the outset because of the relative inefficiency that had plagued their out-of-district transportation programs for years. They had learned of school bus companies who did not comply with federal, state, and local laws, and even suffered through times when bus companies went out of business in the middle of a school year, causing tremendous inconveniences for the school children and their parents. The districts were mindful of the redundancy of effort in managing each of their programs individually. The issues of safety and risk management, cost savings and efficiency, and doing what made perfect sense, all played a role in the establishment of this pupil transportation consortium.

## A TWO-PART COST SAVINGS ANALYSIS

**Management Cost Savings:** Prior to the 1999–2000 school year the four school districts each had at least one staff person engaged in coordinating transportation matters on at least a part-time basis. According to the respective school business officials the aggregate cost of these coordinating services to the districts was $104,678 for the 1998–1999 school year. Table 12.1 outlines the 1998–1999 management costs expensed by each school district in that year.

In the 1999–2000 school year the regional consulting agency is billing the consortium $60,000 for management services. The net manage-

**Table 12.1    Management Costs**

| District | 1998–99 Mgmt. Costs |
|----------|---------------------|
| District A | $ 37,000 |
| District B | $ 18,000 |
| District C | $ 16,678 |
| District D | $ 33,000 |
| **Total** | **$104,678** |

ment cost savings to the districts is $44,678, a 40 percent decrease in costs. With the agency now in place as consortium manager, the staff people originally handling transportation matters have been freed up to perform other duties, allowing each district an opportunity to consolidate and make more efficient its business office operations.

**Contract Cost Savings:** The transportation consortium has reduced the number of contract routes serving out-of-district schools by 25 in the 1999–2000 school year. The total contract cost savings is estimated to be $291,000, a 25 percent decrease in costs. Table 12.2 outlines the year-to-year costs and net first-year savings to each district.

Through efficient routing and stricter management controls, the districts have been able to save a significant amount of money in the first year of the program. The $4,400 per student per year cost has dropped to $2,934 in 1999–2000, a 33 percent decrease. The districts anticipated a cost savings but not to the extent that actually occurred. The fact that savings were so significant generated interest from other school districts in the region who wanted to know how it was accomplished.

The answer lies in the numbers—numbers of children and the power

**Table 12.2    Contract Cost Savings**

| District | 1998–1999 Costs | 1999–2000 Costs | Net Savings | % Savings |
|----------|-----------------|-----------------|-------------|-----------|
| District A | $  175,000 | $135,000 | $  40,000 | 23% |
| District B | $  490,000 | $460,000 | $  30,000 | 8% |
| District C | $  114,000 | $  87,000 | $  27,000 | 24% |
| District D | $  394,000 | $200,000 | $194,000 | 50% |
| **Totals** | **$1,173,000** | **$882,000** | **$291,000** | **25%** |

inherent in strong economies of scale when routing. Having a large pool of children attending the various out-of-district schools allowed for routes that were particularly more efficient in 1999–2000 when compared to previous years.

## EVALUATION: THE DISTRICTS SPEAK OUT

Evaluating the successes of the transportation consortium has invariably resulted in a review of the cost savings. Success stories in school business administration naturally connect to a form of financial achievement, so this is clearly understood. What is noteworthy, though, is the fact that the work of the regional consulting agency has significantly reduced the need for the four districts to handle the mundane, day-to-day activities of their individual school transportation operation. The professional shared transportation office has centralized these operations, brought focus to very specific goals (besides costs savings), and clearly resulted in a safer network of pupil transportation for the children residing in these school districts. Through professional management of transportation contracts and a proactive approach to integrating technology in the transportation office, the regional consulting agency has brought to these districts a state-of-the art pupil transportation management model.

The Superintendent of Schools of District "D" perhaps best summed up what the consortium has meant to all four districts when he stated, "This collective agreement between the four districts is saving time and money that allows us to shift our resources to more educational issues. It's the right thing to do for the taxpayers and it's the right thing to do for the children—and it's working. Many thanks goes to the regional consultant for developing the structure of the consortium and for its professionalism."

## COMMUNICATION: HOW THE CONCEPT WAS COMMUNICATED

The initial discussion about the possibility of creating a pupil transportation consortium was communicated at a meeting of school business officials. The meeting was set up to address the problems that each school district faced regarding their transportation programs, particularly the program in place to transport students to the many out-of-district private, parochial, and special education schools. Subsequently, a written proposal was prepared that outlined exactly what the regional consulting agency was prepared to do for the cooperating school districts. The proposal contained a summary of the services to be provided with specific goals, a cost analysis including projected first-year cost savings, a timeline for program rollout, and an anticipated budget. This proposal was provided to the school business officials and school superintendents, shared with the Boards of Education, and discussed at public meetings.

## CONCLUDING THOUGHTS

The pupil transportation consortium concept is more than just another example of school districts sharing services. It is an innovative approach to meeting a truly significant challenge transporting today's school children safely and cost effectively. The school districts described in this paper truly succeeded in accomplishing the goals initially outlined in their written proposal. They achieved tremendous first-year cost savings that has permitted a greater investment in educational programs that benefit their children. These successes have earned the districts a renewed sense of respect from their Boards of Education and their constituencies. Not surprisingly, this has prompted other school districts in the region to inquire about how they might also benefit from the pupil transportation consortium concept. The concept has a proven record of accomplishment and will likely be used as a model for future school district collaborations in this very important area of school business administration.

# CHAPTER 13

# Primary Vendor Contract for Maintenance Supplies

## Purchasing

Deborah R. Grant
RSBO, Supervisor of Purchasing/Accounts Payable
Independent School District #742
St. Cloud, MN

*CCD District Details: 20 schools; 10,486 students; "Mid-size central city"; 1,605 total staff; 924 "other staff"; total 2001–2002 expenditures: $86 million*

## OVERVIEW OF THE PRACTICE

We instituted just-in-time purchasing of maintenance products from one primary vendor via the competitive bid process. This practice has produced lower costs, better trained staff, reduced inventories, and a safer working environment.

## PURPOSE OF THE PRACTICE

We needed to provide a more efficient method of procuring maintenance supplies. Our objective was to provide custodial staff with product training, reduce building inventory levels and costs, provide management reports to analyze product requirements, provide usage patterns and inventory levels by location, provide monthly ordering and delivery of products, and standardize the maintenance products used in the district.

## COST ANALYSIS OF THE PRACTICE

Our bid specifications called for a two-year contract with an option to renew for two additional years. This contract period required the vendor to make a long-term commitment to the district in return for all of the custodial product business. Purchases during the first year of the contract were 7 percent lower than the previous year. The changes implemented resulted in a decrease in the average cost per square foot of $ .02, equaling a savings of $34,502, after the second year of the contract. Upon contract renewal after two years, prices increased only 3 percent on one product category and 7 percent on another product category out of 38 product categories.

Approximately 174 hours of supervisory, clerical, and custodial time were saved in the first bid and ordering process. By awarding a multi-year contract, approximately 200 hours will be saved on the bidding and ordering process in each subsequent year of the contract. This timesaving allows us to redirect that time to other value-added tasks.

## EVALUATION OF THE PRACTICE

Under the old method of purchasing once a year, we tried to identify all of the items that would be needed by having the custodians submit their estimated needs. There were 248 line items on the bid. We received and evaluated bids from 16 vendors and awarded the bid by line item. The vendor for the estimated annual needs of the district issued separate orders. Each building had to allocate space to store their annual supply needs. All products were paid for at the beginning of the year. We paid higher prices on small reorders when custodians underestimated their building needs. We had overstocks when custodians overestimated their building needs. The head custodian in each of our 21 buildings spent approximately four hours completing an inventory and estimating usage for the following year. The bid evaluation process took a minimum of 24 hours. After the bids were awarded, the product information and actual costs were distributed to each building for preparation of their actual order, consuming another two to three hours of the custodians' time plus a minimum of 40 hours of clerical time.

Under the old process, the actual chemicals purchased year to year often changed. The custodians were constantly getting new products that had new safety handling issues, new dilution ratios, and new application methods. Custodians substituting in one building could be using chemicals that they never used in any other building and they had not been trained on the correct and safe use of that item. Custodians were reluctant to change products once they found one they thought worked the best, however they were often forced to change products when we purchased low-bid items each year. Adding products to our bid list based upon individual custodian preference did not allow us to standardize on products or to maximize our buying power.

An evaluation of the bid and actual usage showed that 50 line items represented 78 percent of total purchases of $80,000. The 50 items were listed in the bid specifications for price comparisons along with the vendor offering a discount on all other items they stock. By switching to just-in-time purchasing, it was no longer necessary for the head custodians to complete an inventory or estimate the needs for the following year, which saved 84 hours on that process. The Quality Control Committee and the Supervisor of Purchasing evaluated bids. The time spent evaluating the bids was reduced to 16 hours. Since orders would be placed as needed, it was no longer necessary for each head custodian to spend two to three hours preparing annual orders or clerical time tabulating needs and preparing orders. A minimum of 174 hours was freed up for more value-added tasks.

Maintenance supply inventories are now under control. Minimum and maximum reorder points have been established in each building. Orders are placed as needed during the contract at firm pricing with next-day delivery. The vendor worked with the custodians to ensure that old stock was used prior to ordering new items. The custodians know that they will be receiving the same product each time they place an order. The vendor provides individual and group training, showing new products and correct product usage. Usage reports are provided by product and by square foot to help identify costs and possible overuse or misuse of products. The Quality Control Committee is currently working to narrow the list of products used in the district that will contribute to a safer working environment. Each product containing chemicals has a corresponding Material Safety Data Sheet detailing the proper use of the product, the hazards of the product, and the necessary actions to be taken in the case of an emergency. To date, approximately 300 products have been eliminated and that means there are fewer chemicals in the schools and 300 less Material Safety Data Sheets to be concerned about.

The primary vendor contract for maintenance supplies has met the objectives that were set for the process and the end users subscribe to the new process.

## HOW THE PRACTICE WAS COMMUNICATED TO COLLEAGUES, THE SCHOOL BOARD, AND THE COMMUNITY

This process represented a paradigm shift in how we purchased maintenance products. Therefore, it was essential to get the custodians to buy into the concept. Meetings were held with the Quality Control Committee, made up of a group of head custodians, to introduce and discuss the process. Once the Quality Control Committee was convinced of the benefits of the process, it was introduced to all of the head custodians. The custodians had ownership in the process, as they helped write the bid specifications for products and services, they were involved in evaluating the bids, and they are involved in the ongoing evaluation of the process.

We have just completed the second year of the program and now have actual results for the primary vendor contract for custodial supplies. I will be sharing the information and results with colleagues during regional and state meetings.

## HOW THE PRACTICE PROMOTES AND ENHANCES THE OVERALL OPERATION OF THE ENTITY

A quality control committee was established within the custodial group. This group has a voice in the products and services that are needed by the district and are stakeholders in the process. Standardization of products allows for more efficient training of staff. Old stocks have been used up, next-day delivery eliminates the over-ordering that often happened when ordering once a year, costs are reduced with firm bid price for the year on all orders, safety issues have been reduced when working with chemicals due to the reduction in the number of items on hand, efficiency is increased when custodians are working with the same products in subsequent years and when working in different buildings, and we are insured of compatibility of products when purchasing from one vendor.

## HOW THE PRACTICE IS INNOVATIVE

There is a certain comfort level in continuing with the same process year after year. Our experienced custodial staff was unsure that a change in process was necessary. The primary vendor contract for maintenance supplies required getting the custodians involved from the beginning as stakeholders and working together to implement a new method of procurement to help them be more efficient in their jobs.

## HOW THE PRACTICE CAN BE IMPLEMENTED BY OTHERS

The primary vendor contract for maintenance supplies can be implemented in other school districts by involving custodians in the process from the beginning and by writing bid specifications that clearly identify the level of products and services required to meet the needs of the district.

# CHAPTER 14

# District Energy Program
# Reaps Multiple Rewards
## Facilities Management, Energy Efficiency

Don Rappold
Assistant Superintendent for Administrative Services
Lewiston Porter Central School District
Youngstown, NY

*CCD District Details: 4 schools; 2,435 students; "Rural"; 365 total staff; 184 "other staff"; total 2001–2002 expenditures: $27 million*

## OVERVIEW

A comprehensive energy conservation program centered on a self-funded energy performance contract with a local energy services company has provided benefits far exceeding all expectations for Lewiston Porter Central School District, a 2,550 student school district. The project, initially the brainchild of the district's Assistant Superintendent for Administrative Services, was initiated primarily to address mounting building system deterioration issues and rising energy costs.

The district, as many others across the country, faced many problems including climbing utility costs, deteriorating buildings and building systems, a very tight operating budget, and the reluctance of local taxpayers to fund capital improvement projects.

The administration was challenged with the problem of addressing serious facility issues with less state funding and minimal commitment from the public. The primary focus was to find a way to convince the

73

public that the district was doing all it could to solve problems with its own resources. In turn, the district hoped to gain support from the public, if they knew that their tax dollars would be spent on cost effective, needed capital improvements.

While addressing these issues directly, the far-reaching benefits of the program have included:

- Annual energy cost savings of $101,000.
- New and upgraded mechanical systems.
- Construction of a state-of-the-art cogeneration system that is viewed by other district's as an example of energy conservation excellence and has significantly reduced the District's dependency on the electric utility industry.
- Taxpayer confidence in the district. This confidence was witnessed in the ultimate support and approval of a $14.8 million district-wide capital improvement program.
- A 10-year partnership with the Energy Performance Contractor that has had numerous mutual benefits.
- Creation of an Energy Education Program for staff and students that is being introduced to support existing curriculums and increase energy efficiency and environmental awareness.

## PURPOSE OF PROGRAM

There were numerous objectives identified for the program, all of which were of significant importance to be able to consider the endeavor a success. The primary goals were as follows:

- Significantly reduce the utility budget for the district, allowing for additional dollars to be spent on direct education expenses.
- Improve safety and environmental conditions in all district buildings.
- Increase public and student awareness of the benefits of energy conservation.
- Improve the operation of the mechanical and electrical system serving the district's buildings.

- Reduce the reliance on public utilities.
- Grow public support for addressing deteriorating building conditions, and indicate that funds are expended in the most cost effective manner possible.
- Build public confidence to a level that would support a much-needed capital improvement project, future budgets, and hopefully a future energy project that would completely make the district energy self-sufficient.

## COST ANALYSIS

The first and most important aspect of the proposed energy program was the completion of a Comprehensive Energy Audit of the district's five educational buildings and Administration Center. Typically, a detailed study of this type can cost $.08/sq. ft. or approximately $49,600 for the district's 620,000 sq. ft. complex.

As these funds were not available in the annual budget, the district applied for a matching grant to the state Energy Research and Development Authority to assist in the audit funding. An incentive of $25,000 was ultimately awarded, with the energy services company absorbing the remaining cost of the study with no direct district or taxpayer expense. The ultimate cost of the energy performance project was $1,525,000 and was financed over a 10-year period through a tax-exempt lease agreement. Energy savings and State Building Aid completely fund the project with a positive cashflow for the district.

## EVALUATION

The program has been extremely effective not only from a cost savings and financial perspective but as the impetus for other direct and indirect benefits including:

- Verified annual energy cost savings in excess of $100,000.
- Reduction in annual building repair expenses.
- Significant improvement in the public's perception of the school

district and its fiscal policies. The district has historically had great difficulty in passing both voter referendum budgets and capital projects. The successful energy performance contract, implemented at no cost to local taxpayers, has convinced residents that the district is pursuing all alternative approaches to minimize local taxes, improve district facilities, and maintain facilities to reduce the magnitude of future capital improvements. The local taxpayers approved in May of 2000 a $14.8 million capital project addressing building structural requirements, data networking improvements, building HVAC, plumbing, and electrical system upgrades.

• The district's renewed interest and understanding of energy efficiency and environmental issues has promoted public support of a totally nondistrict-funded outdoor environmental ecosystem classroom with natural habitat growth, wildlife, and fish for Natural Science Studies.

• The energy services company selected by the district has developed an excellent knowledge of the district's facilities and was later selected to be the on-site project manager for the $14.8 million construction program. The energy services company will have a full-time, on-site representative through the term of the project who is responsible for coordinating construction, maintaining the project schedule, ensuring project safety requirements are followed, and coordinating day-to-day construction tasks with regular school educational and extracurricular activities.

The district and the energy services company have also partnered on the development of an energy education program specifically designed for all students and staff. The program, generally consisting of specific grade-level lesson plans, includes experiments, PowerPoint presentations, contests, poster campaigns, Career Day presentations, and building tours focusing on energy efficiency.

## COMMUNICATION TO COLLEAGUES, SCHOOL BOARD, AND COMMUNITY

The success of the program cannot be gauged in cost savings alone. Of equal importance to the community, Board of Education, and neighboring school districts were the program's overall performance, its innovation, and its applicability to other districts.

Any successful project is contingent on clear and open communication and this project's results are a direct consequence of not only open communication, but sharing input and ideas to ensure that all were thoroughly investigated and incorporated in the program.

Communication of the program was accomplished by several methods including the following:

- An Energy and Facilities Committee was formed that included district administrators, teachers, parents, school board members, and concerned citizens that interfaced with the Energy Services Company to provide input regarding priorities, areas of concern, and the anticipated goals of the project.
- Regular updates were provided to the Board of Education and the community at School Board meetings to address project progress, objectives, schedule, and project performance.
- Following completion, project presentations were provided to the regional Board of Cooperative Educational Services and the project was featured at numerous School Board, Superintendent, Business Official, and Buildings and Grounds Officials conferences and trade shows to convey the project's success and its applicability to similar situations.

## INNOVATION

Many districts have implemented successful energy performance contracts but certain aspects of this project indicate special innovative characteristics as follows:

- Through grants and contract negotiations, the entire project was completed with zero local taxpayer dollars, with all funding from the state, the guarantee of the energy performance contract, and the energy services company.
- Most energy performance contracts involve typical lighting, motor

replacement, and control system measures. This project addressed these areas, but also included a cogeneration system project for the high school building that produces both electricity and thermal energy for the building's domestic hot water, space heating, and swimming pool.

- The partnership formed by the district and the energy services company has developed into a long-term relationship with continuous evolving service provisions that benefit the district.
- The intent of the energy performance contract was to not only reduce operating costs and improve systems' operation, but also gain public support for future capital project referendums.

# CHAPTER 15

# Building Mentoring Program
## Internal Operations, Human Resources

George E. Schenck
Assistant Superintendent—Administration/Finance
Cape Henlopen School District
Lewes, DE

*CCD District Details: 7 schools; 4,145 students; "Rural"; 605 total staff; 315 "other staff"; total 2001–2002 expenditures: $35 million*

## THE PROGRAM

The Cape Henlopen School District was recently labeled as the "Mentoring District." Mentoring has been in existence for almost six years throughout our system and has had a tremendous impact on mentees, mentors, and most importantly the students. Feedback from participants has been upbeat and overwhelmingly positive, with many comments about how much more all employees have been able to accomplish with the assistance of willing colleagues.

Prior to the start of the 1999–2000 school year, the Superintendent and Assistant Superintendent introduced the Board to a new concept, Board Building Mentoring. The new incentive was intriguing to all the members because it had no associated costs, required total district-wide involvement, and offered numerous resultant benefits. The Board viewed it as a wonderful opportunity to augment visibility and communication at all leadership levels.

Expectations and a methodology were developed which could be generically utilized throughout the system. Each of the seven Board members was assigned to be a mentor for one of the seven school sites. Buildings were assigned outside their individual residence areas and at no cost (except extra time) to the district.

Presently the program is thriving and in its second year of existence. At each of our two monthly Board Meetings, time is allotted so each member may share their building experiences. The summaries are uplifting, rewarding, and passionate. Members share information and experiences about teaching, the effectiveness of new programs, content standards, special events, and student successes. The Board is excited about their new role and have become coaches who are totally immersed in the educational process.

This program, along with many other new initiatives, has enabled us to achieve a reputation of educational prominence in our state. As a "Team," we were willing to take a chance! Here is a flourishing major program that has no associated costs. It worked and continues to work! No one will ever be able to accurately measure all the associated successes and good feelings that have been established and continue to develop each day. Perhaps this is the reason why we continue to occupy many of the top positions in the testing program adopted by our state.

## CAPE HENLOPEN SCHOOL DISTRICT BOARD BUILDING MENTORING PROGRAM

Expectations of Program

- To provide the necessary assistance required to establish a positive atmosphere at the individual building level for the implementation of the complex duty of educating children.
- To focus on what is most advantageous for students in the context of student achievement.
- To eliminate feelings of isolation and promote the professional well-being of building employees.
- To provide the opportunity to visit other district schools and/or areas.

- To enhance district-wide communications, establish an atmosphere of collegiality and promote school improvement.
- To establish a spirit of responsibility and support in sharing concerns about the daily challenges of education.
- To develop a thorough understanding of individual building issues and the day-to-day experiences of the building population.
- To encourage the formation of productive developmental changes that foster excellence in teaching.
- To furnish a forum to review current policies, develop fresh ideas and observe the practices being utilized to educate children.
- To offer assistance to new employees.

## PROPOSED METHODOLOGY

- Assignment of Board Members to the mentoring program will be made each July at the monthly workshop meeting. Mentors will serve as building contacts for one year.
- Mentors will be assigned in accordance with their areas of interest. It is recommended that Board Members consider serving as mentors for buildings not located in their residence areas.
- Upon assignment, a contact will be made to arrange an introductory conference to establish mutual expectations for the year and to tour the physical plant.
- Mentors will help facilitate the process of locating community resources to support special building projects/initiatives.
- Mentors are encouraged to attend an assortment of building events and visit as many of the individual classrooms and work sites as possible.
- Meetings at the building level shall be nonjudgmental and characterized by an open environment where questions can be asked freely.
- The primary thrust of each encounter should be upon instructional improvement and the success of students.
- Mentors are to serve as coaches and not evaluators.
- Mentors must be ready to assume many roles. These could include

counselor, coach, sponsor, role model, resource, colleague, sponsor or leader.

- It is expected that the program will not infringe upon the privacy rights of the building employees or students.
- Mentors are encouraged to be a participant in an assortment of curriculum activities. This could include observing a writing lesson, the new math curriculum, a Smithsonian lesson, new building initiatives, etc.
- It is proposed that at least one contact be made between each regularly scheduled meeting of the Board. Unannounced visits are encouraged and are expected to be a standard part of the program.

# CHAPTER 16

# Superintendent's Building Excellence Program
## Facilities Management

Joseph M. Tyo Jr.
Director of Operations & Risk Management
Clover Park School District #400
Lakewood, WA

*CCD District Details: 34 schools; 13,769 students; "Urban fringe of large city"; 1,516 total staff; 780 "other staff"; total 2001– 2002 expenditures: $89 million*

The Superintendent's Building Excellence Program was initially designed to provide a mechanism to evaluate the cleanliness of the district's schools. The district had an inspection program, but the method used did not allow for any comparison of the schools that were checked. The superintendent was very frustrated with a program that did not provide criteria for evaluation and a framework for improvement. The new program is criteria based and measures each building against the same criteria and against the same type of schools, i.e., elementary to elementary, secondary to secondary.

The program was not established to be an inspection program per se, but rather it was advertised as an observation program. School principals are very familiar with observations and that term does not convey the negative connotation that the term inspection carries. It was hoped that the staff would see the observation as a part of the successful program execution of the school. Two observations are scheduled per year, one unannounced and one announced. The two observations are generally about three months apart. Following an observation the schools receive a detailed report outlining the findings of the observation to serve as a guide for future operations.

It became clear to the staff that just looking at the cleanliness of a facility did not maximize the impact of the observation. It was obvious that we could accomplish a much broader overview of the district's facilities. A three-member team that participates in the program at each school conducts all observations. Prior to going to the school the team reviews the building condition code of the facility and the outstanding work orders being held by the Maintenance Department. During the course of the observation the team evaluates the main components of the facility HVAC, structural, etc., to see how they compare to the building condition code. Any discrepancies that are noted are passed on to the District Planning Officer so that he can schedule an evaluation by the appropriate department to update the building condition code.

Prior to initiating the observation the team reviews all of the open work orders being held by the Maintenance Department. A list is then taken to the school and given to the Chief Custodian who compares them to his list of open work orders. While the team is conducting the observation it notes items that they believe should be work orders and compare the findings with the list of confirmed work orders. Items that have not already been submitted are then included in the miscellaneous portion of the report so that the work is placed on the Maintenance work schedule. This process has resulted in better scheduling and a more complete list of the requirements existing in the district and has allowed the district to maximize the efforts of the Maintenance workforce. The observation also serves as a quality control tool to review how the work within the district is being performed. This process has enhanced our ability to track our projects and insure that our money is spent in the best interests of the district.

The purpose behind the program was to ensure cleanliness standards within the district. Once the program began and we started to evaluate what we were doing and looked at what we could do, it became clear that we could observe and evaluate a number of areas in the school, so we modified the program. The redesigned purpose was to evaluate building cleanliness, facility condition, and the status of maintenance work in the building. This gave us an overview of the facility and its programs and a snapshot of the comparative status of the facilities in the district.

The direct cost of this program is minimal to the district. The team is comprised of three members, the Director of Operations and Risk Management, the Supervisor of the Utility Team and the Loss Control Specialist. Elementary observations take two hours to perform and two hours to document. Secondary school observations take four hours and two hours to document. There are 28 facilities in the district, 19 elementary, and 9 secondary facilities. The total hours dedicated to the conduct of the observations are as follows.

- Elementary: 58 hours @ $97.00 per hour = $5,626.00 × 2 observations per year = $11,252.00
- Secondary: 54 hours @ $97.00 per hour = $5,238.00 × 2 observations per year = $10,476.00
- Total personnel costs for the program = $11,252.00 + 10,476.00 = $21,728.00

Since the advent of the program the district has significantly reduced the time that the maintenance department spends tracking work orders. The number of open work orders requiring review has been drastically cut. Normal work order processing time was just over 14 days for a non-emergency work order. The current process has reduced that to just over five working days. The system is more streamlined and user friendly. Site managers have been shown how to access the system on a daily basis to determine the status of outstanding work orders. This has significantly impacted response time. Cost savings are estimated as follows:

- Personnel processing savings 115 hours @ $18.00 per hour = $2,070.00
- Reduction in return visits by the crew 147 hours @ $23.00 = $3,381.00
- Total Quality Control = $5,751.00

Quality control savings $3,750.00 in parts, 87 hours @ $23.00 = $2,001.00

Estimated cost avoidance totaled $167,000, as follows:

- Water leaks at a high school. Early detection of ceiling leak prevented rupture of the coolant lines. Estimated cost of ceiling and line repair from a rupture = $42,000
- Systems freeze in the chilling tower at a high school. Detection of the failure resulted in early preventive maintenance resulting in saving the coil. Cost of replacing the coil = $47,000
- Cracks in urinals at a high school. Sealing these cracks and replacing urinals where required eliminated water leakage into the subflooring of the restroom. Cost to repair or replace the floor = $29,000
- Defective wiring in the library and sewing room at a middle school. Detection of this problem enabled the district to correct the problem and avert a fire or electrocution. Cost savings to the district = $49,000

The district's personnel costs associated with this program are far outweighed by the benefits derived from the program.

The members of the observation team and the administrators responsible for program implementation evaluated the effectiveness of the program throughout its execution. A detailed review of each observation was made to determine the effectiveness of the criteria used during the conduct of the observation, the application of the criteria by the observation team, and the impact to the district in evaluating the status of the facility and the staff. This review resulted in program improvements between the unannounced observation and the announced observation. It was determined that the measuring criteria were far too tight and as a result criteria were modified to provide a better tool for the observation team. The first round of observations was conducted using the original criteria to insure that every site was on the same playing field. The second round of observations was conducted using the new criteria and it became immediately obvious that the modifications made improved the method of observation. As the second round of observations commenced it was evident from the start that significant improvements had been made in the condition and cleanliness of the schools. We further found that the processing time of work orders had been reduced and the backlog of work orders had been reduced. Major systems errors were averted through early detection and the overall morale of the custodial staff increased significantly. It was the district's assessment that this program is having a major impact on the district, the individual sites, and the staff.

The district communicated the components of the program in a notice sent out to principals. The notice process is the official notification system of the district. The superintendent was briefed one-on-one on the start-up of the program and two presentations were made to the board of education. The first presentation was an information briefing and the second presentation was the presentation of Clean Sweep Awards to the top facilities in the first round of observations. The district has also developed a Standard Operating Procedure that has been placed in the district Business Procedures Manual. This SOP outlines the parameters of the program and contains the observation criteria.

Following each evaluation the team sends out a detailed report, complete with photographs, that contains the findings of the observation. The findings of the first report are compared with results from the second observation to determine the work done at the school to correct findings from the first observation. The report serves as a tool to identify the facilities status and to assist the facility to correct findings.

This program could be easily implemented by any district or school organization. Its premise is simple and keyed to providing clean and well-maintained facilities to educate our children. Every district has the stewardship responsibility for its facilities and the Building Excellence Program provides a useful tool to assist in the oversight of organizational facilities. It is the unique collaboration of custodial, maintenance, and risk management oversight that makes this program so complete. The comprehensive approach to facilities overwatch enables the community to track the status of its facilities and to hold the district administration responsible for maintaining its facilities.

The Superintendent's Building Excellence Program has served not only to assist in building maintenance and cleanliness, but has enabled us to identify training shortfalls for our staff. The presentation of awards and the internal competition have raised the level of performance in this district. This program serves as a multiplier in providing a quality learning environment for our students.

## About the Editor

**David Ritchey**, Ph.D., is Director of Government and Public Affairs for ASBO International, Reston, Virginia. He has been with ASBO for more than three years.